TEACHING LITERATURE IN TIMES OF CRISIS

T0384789

Teaching Literature in Times of Crisis looks at the range of different crises currently affecting students – from climate change and systemic racism, to the global pandemic.

Addressing the impact on students' ability and motivation to learn as well as their emotional wellbeing, this volume guides teachers toward strategies for introducing both canonical and contemporary literature in ways that demonstrate the future relevance of sophisticated and targeted literacy skills. These reading practices are invaluable for framing and critically examining the challenges associated with crisis in order to help cope with grief and as a means to impart the skills needed to deal with crisis, such as adaptability, flexibility, resilience, and resistance. Providing necessary background theory, alongside practical case studies, the book addresses:

- Reading practices for demonstrating how literature explores ethical issues in specific and concrete rather than abstract terms
- Making connections between disparate phenomena, and how literature mobilises affect in individual and collective human lives
- Supporting teachers in considering new, imaginative ways students can learn from literary content and form in online or remote learning environments, as well as face to face
- Combining close and distant reading with creative and hands-on strategies, presenting the principles of a transitional pedagogy for a world in flux.

This book introduces teachers to methods for reading and studying literature with the aim of strengthening and promoting resilience and resourcefulness in and out of the literature classroom and empower students as global citizens with local roles to play.

Sofia Ahlberg is Vice Dean of the Faculty of Languages at Uppsala University, Sweden, with responsibility for education and collaboration. She teaches and researches on contemporary literature, pedagogy, and ecocriticism.

TEACHING LITERATURE IN TIMES OF CRISIS

Sofia Ahlberg

Routledge
Taylor & Francis Group

LONDON AND NEW YORK

First published 2021
by Routledge
2 Park Square, Milton Park, Abingdon, Oxon OX14 4RN

and by Routledge
605 Third Avenue, New York, NY 10158

Routledge is an imprint of the Taylor & Francis Group, an informa business

© 2021 Sofia Ahlberg

British Library Cataloguing-in-Publication Data
A catalogue record for this book is available from the British Library

Library of Congress Cataloging-in-Publication Data
A catalog record has been requested for this book

ISBN: 978-0-367-63801-6 (hbk)
ISBN: 978-0-367-63799-6 (pbk)
ISBN: 978-1-003-12074-2 (ebk)

Typeset in Bembo
by Taylor & Francis Books

For my students

CONTENTS

ACKNOWLEDGEMENTS

I am grateful for the support and friendship I received at the Department of English, Uppsala University, during the process of writing this book. I am deeply indebted to the mentorship I have received from friends and colleagues both near and far. We have shared coffee and semlor in Stockholm and fika in Uppsala's Katedralskolan. There have been many stimulating phone calls in and out of hours, kindness, and festivity over Zoom. Thanks also to new colleagues at the Faculty leadership for allowing me to learn from them about the inner workings of the university while I was writing this book. Most of all I thank all of the students who have so generously shared with me their own curiosity and passion for discovery. They are too many to list by name, but Emelie Johansson deserves a special mention for alerting me to the pedagogical possibilities of rabbit holes and canine companions. And it was Erik Skogh who first suggested that I write a book about how to study literature in the classroom. I want to offer my warmest thanks to Niamh Ni Shiadhail who inspired me to focus my research in the area of pedagogy and innovative approaches to teaching and learning at a time when I was facing a turning point in my professional life. Niamh, thank you for your counsel. This book is written with your words of wisdom in mind. Many thanks must go to Sue Ericson who put me on the road to Eldforsen where the bulk of this book was written. Apart from that, I owe much gratitude to the soundness of your observations, the breadth of your perspective, and the laughter you provoke at our end of the corridor. I also owe many thanks to the anonymous readers of my initial proposal for this book. Their comments emboldened me to take some ideas further while avoiding unnecessary pitfalls. Thank you also to Polly Dodson at Routledge for your encouragement and belief in this book project.

This book communes with a large company of fellow readers and teachers who have taught me the lesson embodied by moss, a species said to give more to its environment than it takes. My first English teacher in Kinshasa, Mr Riddle, proved that literature can heal a broken heart. Mr Powers, during my first IB year, showed me that everything I learned was political. At Melbourne University, Dr Helene Nevola needed only to notice me to turn me into a scholar. Also at Melbourne, Dr Grace Moore, my doctoral supervisor, reminded me that I can be both a mother and a scholar. And from La Trobe University, friend and colleague Terry Eyssens has been exemplary for his patient commitment to learning from and writing to country at Wehla. While working on this book, I have been uplifted by the wild teachings and sagacity of my sister Annika Lifh. I also wish to thank my twin brother Joel Ahlberg whose work in conflict resolution has been an inspiration. Finally, without the love, care, and devotion of my beloved fellow brain-stormer Nick Sergeant this book would not be all that it is – his cover photograph "Thin Ice #5" testifies to one of his many talents. Finally, my two children, Ayva and Albin, have given joy and laughter at regular intervals whenever I looked up from the writing of this book to discover what only they could show me.

INTRODUCTION

Social and cultural contexts

In its current usage, the noun *crisis* is often regarded as synonymous with disaster or calamity, sometimes even referring to a situation that is beyond control. However, a more nuanced understanding of the word draws on its origin in the Ancient Greek κρίνω (krīnō) which has meanings including decision, discernment, and judgment. And so a more precise meaning of the word refers generally to "a decisive stage where change must occur" and, in medical terms, "a turning point in a disease." In either sense, change can be for better or for worse. In this book, I emphasise this in order to underscore the importance of teaching students how to engage with crisis rather than regard it as a diagnosis with only a fatal outcome. For example, the way the unfolding environmental and climate crisis is reported often produces anxiety, anger, eco-depression, and overwhelming grief, among the young especially (Wals 2015). Inadequate curricula are not the only problem here. Students face narratives in the press and in social media that present crises such as climate change or the pandemic as unsolvable problems with pessimistic outcomes. To rectify this, the aim of this book is to show teachers how to inspire students to look at radical change and related socio-economic shifts as processes that are unfolding and amenable to their input. Key to my approach is to encourage the development of that discernment or capacity to distinguish or to make a decision that lies at the root of the word crisis.

The aim of the book is therefore to show teachers how they can harness the imagination of students in the classroom for learning about crisis in ways that go beyond doom and gloom scenarios whilst also being realistic in outlook. As a course book, *Teaching Literature in Times of Crisis* is intended to provide teachers with reasons and resources for using literary form and content to help students understand and respond to global crises. In this section, I present the reasons and the theories that underpin the methodology used in the four case studies which illustrate practical ways to engage with literature when decisive change is upon us.

It is not necessary to read the entire book in a sequential order. Readers who want to skip to the hands-on hints and suggestions for how to teach literature in the classroom in times of crisis, please feel free to skip ahead to the case studies for ideas that you can apply to those books (and those like them) in focus. Or, if you would like to be supported in remote teaching strategies emerging from the ongoing Covid-19 crisis, then you might like to skip to the last part of this Introduction. There, in the section "Best practices for emergency remote teaching," I give direct and creative advice for fostering engagement among students whom we as teachers cannot meet face-to-face.

Arguably, literature is always a response to crisis, or an attempt to register its complexity. There are as many forms of crisis as there are literary forms that can deliver insights into its processes. Literature and crisis have many parallels because the narratives that are widely read and that endure involve tension, dramatic turns of events, lessons triumphantly learned or tragically unheeded – just like real-world crisis. What is of most interest for our context is that the tensile creativity that uses a strong desire to tell a story and overcomes or transmutes the confusion and doubt that writers deal with, this literary invention, imparts a corresponding resilience and resourcefulness to attuned readers. And just as narrative rhythm is paced alternately slow and fast, crisis includes both acute and chronic aspects and phases. Climate change is an example of a chronic crisis developing over a prolonged period, as Rob Nixon's writing on slow violence attests. This is true even though specific weather events bring acute impact to localised areas. We could say the same of the technological revolution, the pressure to be changed by it, or to resist that pressure, has both chronic and acute phases. The recent global protests over racial injustice focused in the Black Lives Matter movement are an acute eruption but with centuries-old roots in the African slave trade.

We should be translating skills learned in the literature classroom to real-world purposes. The underside of this is that public narratives can also hinder or obscure creative responses to crisis. The language used to describe and discuss crisis often circumscribes the range of possible options presented to people and this can create separate problems. For example, the changing social relations due to the Covid-19 pandemic focused on the unfortunate phrase "social isolation" which does nothing to dispel the resulting loneliness and alienation. Physical isolation is required to help prevent the disease from spreading, but this does not need to mean we must in fact be socially distant from each other. From a teacher's point of view, creative solutions need to be found to make possible an online community in place of a physical classroom. Language similarly determines the different responses or emphases available to climate change activism as can be gathered just from the names of two of the movements themselves, from Greenpeace (founded 1971) to Extinction Rebellion (founded 2018). A glance at their respective websites shows that each addresses its audience with a very distinct rhetoric. These vastly different attitudes and approaches to crisis point towards the complex meaning of crisis itself.

Rather than attempt a definition, let me flag some assumptions about crisis that underpin the discussions in this book:

- Crisis is fluctuating
- There is both knowledge and ignorance in crisis – no individual or group has all the right answers
- Crisis makes it difficult to separate what *is* from what *was*
- A crisis is often the result of a process that started long ago
- A crisis is made of forces beyond the control of one individual
- While a crisis is never just personal, its impact on an individual can be life-altering

Crisis can be thought of as a tipping point in which things can either improve or deteriorate, as suggested by the etymological origins of the word and precise usage. So it is fair to regard crisis as a powerful departure point for change; it is a stage that demands clear-sighted discernment and balanced judgment of those facing it. As part of their work teaching critical feminist science literacy, Rosa Costa and Iris Mendel conclude that crisis can be understood as "a congestion of ongoing social contradictions" that also involve "contested processes that allow for new forms of domination as well as for new forms of critique and resistance" (81). What does this emphasis on contestation and contradiction involving "new forms of critique and resistance" mean when we talk about reading literature in times of crisis? First of all, it suggests that crisis is a condition affecting all aspects of sociality. It is present in the literature classroom as well as in student readers and thus it will appear, subtly or explicitly, in the ways that texts are interpreted. It may also be thematised within a text that was written during this or a comparable crisis. Importantly, however, with proper guidance the reader is not overwhelmed by the imposing presence of crisis in the world and in the reading experience. This is in large part because the reader is situated in relation to many other readers and emerges as a reader in dialogue with them and able to benefit from their many perspectives. Thus, crisis alters the locus of learning away from the individual (although a crisis is often painfully felt by the individual) to the community (past, present, and future) with whom readers enter into dialogue. The dialogic approach is also reflected in this book, the sum of a number of conversations with colleagues from the Australian and the Swedish tertiary systems and many hours of being, teaching, practising, observing, listening, and learning in the classroom, both digital and physical.

By foregrounding reading as a method of fostering specific futures (while forestalling others), this book is organised around case studies derived from textual couplings that pair traditional works with contemporary texts that are responding to social transformation. Thus, this book guides teachers towards strategies for introducing both canonical and contemporary literature in ways that demonstrate the future relevance of sophisticated and targeted literacy skills in a world subject to crises including extreme climate change and social upheaval. Times of social change require critical reflection and this is best achieved by demonstrating the links between theory and practice, thought and emotion, as well as word and deed. For literary studies, this means learning to show students how reading and reflecting on works from *Alice in Wonderland* (1865) by Lewis Carroll to solarpunk can provoke change in the worldview of readers sufficient to motivate intervention in actual events. I say "intervention" because it draws attention to the continuities between language, literature, and the world as well as the opportunities through the means of language to contribute to events even by resisting or modifying them.

Although the scale of global events places them beyond the power of most individuals to significantly affect them, the major part of our access to these events is via narrative, fictional or not, and so critical literacy offers some command over how to interpret crisis. Another way of saying this is that you are always reading the world. This world is mobilised via literary means so narrative's power is not just descriptive, it can also form part of feedback loops that promote change. At the core of this project is the heartfelt belief that literature's survival through turbulent periods matters, not because of any intrinsic value that makes it distinct from this messy world, but rather because of its manner of connecting readers and writers with the world. I am convinced of literature's capacity to enlist or entangle the energies of a reader to become engaged with the actual or possible world described although readers benefit greatly if given suitable guidance.

The possibility of social transformation lies in the relation with and responsibility towards others. In accord with this, the exercises proposed in this book assume that the principles of dialogue are the foundation of transformative teaching. This obliges us not only to teach students how to read and understand literature but to mentor them in talking back to a text by coming up with their own interpretation. As a cohort, they also thrive on learning the many ways they may share their views with each other and eventually with the scholarly community if that is their ambition. As teachers, we also need to overcome the monologic oppression of prejudicial, oppressive, or even grand narratives. As Australian scholar Deborah Bird Rose explains it, "our postmodern condition is one of failed master narratives; we no longer desire the great stories that once may have made sense of the world for us." Importantly, she says this is "because we have been required to understand the violence they conceal" (24). This suggests a clear role for literary studies, not to try to return to that time of grand narratives but to return to stories and to invent ways of reading them, of dialoguing with them and other readers so as to co-create new meaning for each other. "Dialogue works counter to monologic separatism," says Rose, "it requires a 'we' who share a time and space of attentiveness, and who bring our moral capabilities into the encounter" (30).

Running counter to the idea of social transformation is the sense that a crisis is an interruption to business as usual and that once it is dealt with we will return to the way things were. Instead of this, the emphasis here is on a forward-looking means of encountering times of upheaval that seeks a way through rather than attempting to backtrack. This is because if we insist that crisis is something that we must simply overcome, in the same way that many hope to return to how life was before the Covid-19 pandemic, we lose sight of an opportunity to learn and grow from times that are out of joint. Rose's thoughts on the altogether new process of decolonisation of previously colonised societies are equally relevant to many other social endeavours taken up in times of crisis that need to move forward even when tempted to look back. When working through the unprecedented, "when we have no models from the past to guide us," explains Rose, "we cannot theorise in advance just how it will happen and still be committed to the process" (24). For Rose, it is important to be mindful of the fact that "there is no former time/space of wholeness to which we might return or which we might resurrect for ourselves …. Nor is there a posited future wholeness which may yet save us." This suggests that crisis is an ongoing process rather than an interruption of normality. Our role is to prepare students for futures that differ radically from the past and present. In times of crisis, it is important to give students the means to reflect on cultures of change and the skills to effect change themselves. One of our tasks will be to understand the assumptions we as an educational community make about what of the past should be preserved and what we need to do differently.

Crisis is characterised by misgivings and feelings of doubt regarding past certainties. Our task as teachers has been accurately described by Anne B. Reinertsen as being one that must involve fostering in students "a willingness to work with uncertainty" ("Becoming Earth" 4). In the service of this, Reinertsen writes more like a Beat poet rapping than an academic pedagogue. She recommends teaching students to countenance "dilemmas and paradoxes," including *dissensus* as opposed to the conformity of "consensus which may even constrain learning and change." Note that this eschewal of the need for consensus is not the end of collaboration and dialogue but fertile ground of its flourishing. As Reinertsen indicates in her fascinating, polyvocal introduction to a groundbreaking collection of essays on posthuman pedagogy, individual voices thrive by engaging and resonating with each other. Below, I return to the importance of accepting doubt or uncertainty in the section headed "Horizons of possibilities" when discussing Fumiyo Kagawa and David Selby's method.

Once again, it is in dialogue with others that we develop a collaborative competency which is particularly important in times of crisis in order to promote cooperation rather than fear and suspicion. In the 2018 UNESCO document "Issues and Trends in Education for Sustainable Development," A. Lecht et al. define collaborative competency as being in the service of participatory problem solving, including the ability to learn from others and to understand and respect their needs, perspectives, and actions. This assumes empathy and empathic leadership, the ability to understand, relate to, and be sensitive to others especially when dealing with conflicts in a group. With uncertainty comes a greater need for care. In their article about enhanced student learning through engagement and care in higher education, Robyn Barnacle and Gloria Dall'Alba note that the first step is "for students and teachers to want to be receptive to the other" (1330). As teachers, they suggest, we must model how to care and develop this capacity among our students, "not only in terms of promoting passion for ideas and objects, but also through students caring about each other in their interactions" (1333).

It is perhaps obvious from the discussion so far that the kind of engagement in times of crisis for students and teachers comes with an increased sense of risk taking, breaking out of preconceptions, going beyond our limits, and building patience as we seek new pathways for doing English in the classroom. Often this means embarking on creative and intellectual inquiries that involve mistakes, errors, and false starts. Crisis means reconsidering the past, creating the conditions for something new while living with the contradictions and the mess associated with enduring traces of the past. Donna Haraway famously calls this "staying with the trouble" in a book of the same name. The phrase is her way of referring to the highly complex nature of human and non-human life in our present era. All of this suggests the need to engage rather than retreat from challenges, even more so in times of crisis. With that in mind, teachers will need to be coached to lead class discussions in which students need assistance in struggling with uncomfortable questions, even though that important work is beyond the scope of this book.

During times of crisis, the classroom is likely to be a place in which discussions will relate back to current events and this book reminds teachers of the importance of creating a congenial learning community where such discussions can take place. As social justice educators Brian Arao and Kristi Clemens have discovered, their work "often requires the very qualities of risk, difficulty, and controversy that are defined as incompatible with safety" (139).[1] For them, the term "brave space" works as a way of preparing the ground for a type of discussion that may open up conversations and disrupt as well as decentre "dominant narratives in which knowledge flows one way from teachers to students" (143). Moreover, they suggest agreeing to a set of ground rules at the start of a class or a term. Rules may include "agree to disagree," "don't take things personally," "challenge by choice," "respect," and "no attacks" (143). A classroom characterised as brave space accords with the acceptance of vulnerability proposed by bell hooks in her book *Teaching to Transgress* (1994). For hooks, such a classroom is a place where teachers grow and where "empowerment cannot happen if we refuse to be vulnerable while encouraging students to take risks" (21). This ability to share fragility is important to hooks when practising what she calls liberatory pedagogy which aims to "deconstruct the way power has been traditionally orchestrated in the classroom, denying subjectivity to some groups and according it to others" (139).

Because crisis is deeply felt on a personal as well as a collective level, a starting point in education is to recognise, as Henry Giroux suggests, the need for "pedagogy in which artists, educators, and other cultural workers are neither afraid of controversy nor a willingness to make connections between private issues and broader elements of society's problems" ("Educated Hope"). Giroux's call for justice and engaged dialogue in the classroom has been the subject of many articles and books before the outbreak of the pandemic, although it seems that the response to Covid-19 brings together his scholarly work as evident in the title of a forthcoming book, *Race, Politics, and Pandemic Pedagogy: Education in a Time of Crisis*. In a critical pedagogy manifesto published in 2014, he refers to a pedagogy of repression as what defines students largely by their shortcomings rather than by their strengths, and in doing so convinces them that the only people who know anything are the experts – increasingly drawn from the ranks of the elite and current business leaders, who embody the new models of leadership under the current regime of neo-liberalism.

("Manifesto" 494)

Such pedagogy of repression, Giroux cautions, has now gathered in strength with the emergence of a "pandemic pedagogy" designed to "further a modern-day pandemic of loneliness and alienation" ("Educated Hope"). In his struggle against this, he calls for a pedagogical practice that "does not mould, but inspires, and at the same time it is directive, capable of imagining a better world, the unfinished nature of agency, and the need to consistently re-imagine a democracy that is never finished" ("Educated Hope"). Like bell hooks, Giroux emphasises a two-way dialogue and shared appreciation of vulnerability in the classroom at the heart of which is the notion that teachers must not only educate their students, "but also learn from them" ("Manifesto" 495).

This democratising practice which blurs the distinction between teacher and student is also reflected in cultural theory when it critiques assumed authority. In his essay "The Death of the Author," Roland Barthes famously underscores the emancipatory aspects of reading as an attempt to run counter to the forces of commodification and consumption of the 1960s. Here Barthes argues for a dialogic process of textual interpretation that acknowledges that

text is made of multiple writings, drawn from many cultures and entering into mutual relations of dialogue, parody, contestation but there is one place where this multiplicity is focused and that place is the reader, not as was hitherto said, the author.

(148)

While Barthes does not see the author as the originator of a textual production, he does allow for some kind of originality in the reader as long as this response is not taken to be the one and only reading. *Teaching Literature in Times of Crisis* is inspired by this Barthesian project of reader empowerment not least in how it emphasises the importance of learning as a dynamic and social participation process.

Where Barthes at times ends up exalting literary consumption, and of a rather profligate kind, since the ideal reader does not simply devour a text but somehow assimilates or encounters all of its multiple being, this book situates the student-reader within a participatory framework that fosters a shared knowledge base, a community of practice and established processes for joint reflection and debate. For Jean Lave and Etienne Wenger, learning is foremost an aspect of social practice and as such it "involves the whole person" (53). For them it is not enough to suggest that learning implies a relation to social communities, but indeed "becoming a full participant, a member, a kind of person" as "the activities, tasks, functions, and understandings" that the learner engages with "are part of broader systems of relations in which they have meaning" (53). Thus, they see the participatory framework consisting of these relations on a broader scale:

> These systems of relations arise out of and are reproduced and developed within social communities, which are in part systems of relations among persons. The person is defined by as well as defines these relations. Learning thus implies becoming a different person with respect to the possibilities enabled by these systems of relation. To ignore this aspect of learning is to overlook the fact that learning involves the construction of identities.
>
> *(53)*

Even though the Barthesian project underlies many didactic principles of this book, it is also the case that I see the participatory framework as an important extension of Barthes' dictum expressed in "The Death of the Author." For me, the classroom is the place and context for taking his ideas further by suggesting that reading literature is communal rather than solitary. This is all the more true in times of crisis. Covid-19 has demonstrated to us that the danger of a crisis lies in the fact that it disempowers us by isolating us from each other and from the kind of membership of society that Lave and Wenger argue is crucial for learning. This isolation makes it all the more difficult to imagine life after a crisis since without the power to connect to one another we won't have the power to rebuild a fractured society. The discourse of literary studies assists in providing the kind of language necessary to connect, empower, and rebuild. Lest any reader should suspect that I here employ a rigid definition of community that defines the student of literature in a particular way that sets them apart from the rest, this is far from what I have in mind. Instead, I agree wholeheartedly with Lave and Wenger's definition of community in which openness to difference and diversity is integral:

> We assume that members have different interests, make diverse contributions to activity, and hold varied viewpoints. In our view, participation at multiple levels is entailed in membership in a community of practice. Nor does the term community imply necessarily co-presence, a well-defined, identifiable group, or socially visible boundaries. It does imply participation in an activity system about which participants share understandings concerning what they are doing and what that means in their lives and for their communities.
>
> *(98)*

The aim of the activities presented in *Teaching Literature in Times of Crisis* is to support best classroom practice for enhanced delivery of literature curricula relevant to times of crisis. Key to my expanded reading of Lave and Wenger's notion of "community of practice" – beyond their framework of traditional skills acquisition such as via apprenticeships – is their further remarks such as that it is "an intrinsic condition for the existence of knowledge" as well as, most importantly, "a set of relationships amongst persons, activity, and world" (98). The crisis pedagogy that I demonstrate in this book acknowledges that during a crisis many aspects of a community of practice may be under pressure. And so the practical suggestions contained here aim more often to impart the skills necessary for building or repairing those essential relationships via the activity of reading and writing.

My book is an attempt to reignite a passion for literary studies as being responsive to real-world issues including climate crisis, socio-political upheaval, systemic discrimination based on race, ethnicity or sexual orientation. Teachers are essential for bridging the gap between literary fiction and events unfolding in the world. Thus, I believe that the future legitimacy of the study of literature lies squarely within its close ties to teacher training programmes but only if the research field of both the literary scholar and the work of the educator are productively integrated to produce new knowledge of direct relevance to both. In other words, research needs to be more cognizant of crisis conditions and its didactic potential should be a defined feature of its aims. In this respect, I agree with Leon Botstein's argument that "the dichotomy between research and teaching is false" (76).

Certain questions are of immediate importance for this conjoined effort to make visible the overlap between the theoretical and the practical in times of instability. They include the establishment of a solid, thorough research base to support and inform the work required to translate literary theory into the curricula, as well as the need to examine the implications of literacy understood more broadly as an intrinsic part of engaging with crisis. This book is an attempt to interweave the theoretical and the practical with a method of reading that is based on literary theory as applied to classroom practices. The importance of critical thinking and creativity in times of crisis cannot be underestimated if we appreciate that crisis is a point in time which calls for conscious engagement and measured rather than reflexive or reactive action. Reading practices are integral to the development of critical literacy as they question hegemony, analyse normativity, and promote systems thinking and critique of routines. Next, I will outline some general principles and methods for developing these skills in the literature classroom.

Literary contexts

This section will show how my chosen texts and authors connect to each other within the broader context of crisis and collapse, often doing so via perennial themes. That said, the literary themes are in themselves not what guide the case studies in this book. Rather, my interest is in offering a range of strategies for reading and studying literature in ways that respond to a changing and often volatile world. I have structured these under three headings that broadly define the areas in which I seek to develop literary competency:

Authenticity and enduring understandings
Vital connections between reading, writing, and living
Horizons of possibilities

I think of the above as valuable learning outcomes promoting collaboration, exploration, and attentiveness to the complexity of events in view as well as out of sight. The last point refers to the capacity to see what is going on in one's immediate surroundings, including the actions and reactions of others, within a more generalised awareness of the wider context. Both forms of attention involve forms of reading the world, textually and otherwise. These competencies – born of the study of literature – are the basis for engaging with crisis locally in a continuous and sustained way that is informed by the bigger picture and can possibly affect it as well. This approach to curriculum is geared towards the way a literary work can form the foundation of a renewed appreciation of the complexity of the world with an emphasis on social and natural relationships, collaborative thinking about and responding to literature in the classroom, as well as a willingness to empower students with literary insights that may challenge them to design alternative futures.

Authenticity and enduring understandings

Since the outbreak of Covid-19 in March 2020, when a large majority of teachers around the world were forced to abandon their physical classrooms for emergency remote teaching, education has undergone the most radical change since the transformation of higher education around the time of the industrialisation of society.[2] For many, this has meant learning and using new delivery methods and technologies, perhaps for the first time. Lesson plans, assignments, and assessments have been hurriedly adapted and often without a contingency plan. Teacher support groups have advised it may be necessary to let go of lesson plans as a way of coping with the extra teaching loads due to online teaching and supporting distressed students. As Associate Professor of communication Amy Young put it in a compendium published by *The Chronicle of Higher Education* at the height of the pandemic in 2020, "Decide what students really need to know, and prioritize that" (qtd in Field 10). Young's advice is sound, but easier said than done, especially when under extreme pressure. In their book *Understanding by Design* (2005), Wiggins and McTighe remind us of the importance of clearly defining "enduring understandings" when putting together expected outcomes for a course (qtd in Richardson 17–22). By enduring understandings they mean "the underlying concepts, principles, and processes that are central to a subject or topic" (30).

Once teachers are clear about what these may be, they advise that all course deliverables "should be logically inferred from the results sought, not derived from the methods, books, and activities with which we are most comfortable" (14). With their method of starting at outcomes and working backwards through a range of resources and techniques to come up with suitable pedagogical approaches to support those outcomes, Wiggins and McTighe show the way to make learning more authentic and result-driven. Note that authentic is different from simply being relevant, which is also important. This is because authenticity is a quality of the teaching as well as of the curriculum and it is needed for enlisting student buy-in especially during trying times. For those of us who teach literary studies, authenticity often overlaps with the personal and so we expect our students to make connections between what they read and their experience of the world they live in. We also expect them to be personally affected by what they read. And we need not hide our own stake in the texts we care about nor be embarrassed if our views are not fashionable. For Michael Young, this is precisely what makes literature and the arts "powerful knowledge" because they "engage with feelings such as guilt, remorse, regret, responsibility and joy" (109).

It is worth noting that the nature of literature's enduring understandings is very different during times of relative stability. For example, when readers do not perceive an immediate, discernible threat to their wellbeing, they may believe it is possible or even desirable to detach ethics from aesthetics when doing textual analysis. It would then perhaps seem legitimate to read Virginia Woolf as a stylist of Modernist representations of subjectivity without reflecting deeply on the significance of war or calamity for her characters. William Faulkner might then appear as an ingenious inventor of narrative voices without the need to explore what those voices have to say about the historical fate of the South in the United States. Similarly, during times of stability, readers and students of literature may be swayed by arguments that the value of literature lies squarely within poetics, as argued by Marjorie Perloff among others. By contrast, during times of great instability, students are more likely to focus on narrative as a didactic tool that can offer perspective on and insight into their own times, as well as survival skills or even day-to-day coping strategies. Nevertheless, the understandings that emerge during peace-time may well be relevant in war-time. I believe crisis underscores one of literature's primary enduring understandings, that it is a space of discovery, an enabler of remarkable literary encounters with the new. And this can be fostered either within a didactic framework or with an emphasis chiefly on aesthetics. Indeed, it seems there has never been a more urgent need for the life-long guidance students can get from Wiggins and McTighe's enduring understandings, nor has the role of literary studies been more relevant in providing that guidance.

At the heart of my approach to learning is student engagement and I endorse any method that displays the authenticity that gets students to back it. I have sought student involvement even at the start of designing a course such that students in effect became co-authors of the syllabus. In her book *The New Education: How to Revolutionize the University to Prepare Students for a World in Flux*, Cathy Davidson includes a section based on "ten tips for transforming any classroom for active, student-centered learning." An example of this is that she can leave the room on the first day of class so as to allow the students to structure, organise, and design the course themselves (266). At my own institution, Uppsala University, the Center for Environment and Development Studies (CEMUS) is a student-initiated and student-run centre with a focus on sustainability and equity. Established in 1996, the centre's main focus on inter-disciplinary courses on global survival grew out of David Orr's landmark essay "What is Education For?" in which he calls for a more holistic and integrated understanding of education in relation to the world. As is the case with many other inter-disciplinary centres that sit outside traditional faculties and departments, CEMUS showcases innovative teaching methods that facilitate active student participation on the understanding that students at all levels of their studies can and should be granted responsibility for their own learning. An insight I draw from them that I try not to forget is that as educators we are helping to produce future citizens and decision-makers and thus a feature of my approach is that it helps to identify and foster agency.

Student empowerment is the focus of a number of recently published book-length studies. Karyn Cooper and Robert White's volume *Democracy and Its Discontents: Critical Literacy Across Global Contexts* (2015) helps lay the foundations for thinking about literacy and democracy. Cook-Sather, Bovill and Felten focus on student–faculty partnerships in *Engaging Students as Partners in Learning and Teaching: A Guide for Faculty* (2014). They give guidelines for how to structure curriculum so as to allow students "to engage in democratic practices as well as democratic ways of being" (128). There is much to admire in these and other approaches to student-centred learning, but at the same time they assume that society is relatively stable and the days and weeks of a course more or less uninterrupted by calamity such as socio-political chaos, forced mobility, or even bloodshed. When they speak of crisis, as with Davidson's opening chapter "Quarter-Life Crisis" in *The New Education*, they often mean a crisis within higher education and a university system hopelessly out of touch with the require-ments faced by their students who graduate from university ill-prepared for the real world. During turbulent times, by contrast, what is held to be the real world is often a subject of heated debate if not violent dispute, as evident in the recent presidential election in the United States. Under these conditions, the content of literature courses that strive to be relevant is put under pressure to relate to often conflicting demands of radically changing public discourse.

As a direct result of recent such conflict, the obedient attendance of school children at school is no longer guaranteed. Following student protests beginning in September 2019 with the school strike for climate movement initiated by Swedish 17-year-old Greta Thunberg (#FridaysForFuture), the way knowledge is disseminated has been affected as even school administrators must bow to demands from students (and par-ents) that they be given time off school to attend rallies. What is taught and how to teach it must also adapt to these conditions. Even in courses that do not take the environment as a primary content it may become obligatory to ensure that it is not overlooked and should probably be accorded more than passing attention. Further than that, when teaching Jack Kerouac's *On the Road*, for example, we would acknowledge and explain the heavy use of petroleum that supports this road journey as pilgrimage. Such an approach would be to "sort texts according to the energy sources that made them possible," as suggested by Patricia Yaeger in a 2011 PMLA editorial "Literatures in the Ages of Wood, Tallow, Coal, Whale Oil, Gasoline, Atomic Power, and Other Energy Sources" (305). Another form of energy – African slavery – is highlighted by the recent foregrounding of the Black Lives Matter movement and worldwide protests in the wake of the murder of African-American George Floyd during an arrest in Minneapolis on 25 May 2020. With global protests against police brutality targeting black people that followed this event, how should we teach

Whitman's *Leaves of Grass* as a message of radical inclusivity while knowing of the poet's racist remarks elsewhere?

Even if not responding to these particular questions, the book will demonstrate to teachers the value of mobilising a range of literacies within a context of great social transformation. Teachers of literature at the undergraduate tertiary level will learn ways of using literature in the classroom to provoke reflection and debate on the kind of people and societies their student cohorts might need to become in order to weather the social impact of transition. Through a sequence of empowering reading practices with fresh learning outcomes together with practical advice on how to focus student engagement, the book will help instructors to make pedagogical sense of crisis. This can help them shed light on the way reading methods enable readers to take part in socio-cultural change. Case Study One, "Discovering the Weird and the Wonderful in a Changing World," looks at novels at the heart of which is the quest motif. These include *Alice's Adventures in Wonderland*, Butler's *Parable of the Sower*, and VanderMeer's *Annihilation*, the first book of his *Southern Reach* trilogy. These novels and other quest novels encourage an open-ended exploration geared towards the way a literary work can form the foundation of a renewed appreciation of the complexity of the world with an emphasis on social and natural relationships. I argue here (and elsewhere) that in times of crisis, students need to be reminded that they have the means to enact the change they want to see. Reading a text aloud, or moving that reading into the world, as I will show, are ways of demonstrating that as readers we do not stand outside the text and apart from the world, but rather we are part of it. The text enlists our sympathies and as such it writes us by performing something in us that can change us. This suggests that we become better observers by learning to see what connects us to what we observe. It teaches us that in times of crisis there is little to be gained by the practice of othering, or perceiving a problem as completely separated from myself or my actions.

Vital connections between writing, reading, and living

Teachers support the development of enduring understandings that can be identified in relation to literary works by encouraging students to consider potential parallels between their own emotions and those of the characters in the text and to more generally foster connections between reading and living. An underlying premise of this book is that reading is a far from isolated activity. Rather, there is a vital connection between reading and living, reading and knowing the world, reading and discovering the world, as well as reading and intervening in the world. In times of radical change, the imaginary is our only way of grasping vastly complex and challenging phenomena. My belief is that only narrative can adequately frame what is happening so that it can be discussed and debated. Importantly, narrative is not just used by authors of fiction but also by scientists, politicians, journalists, documentary filmmakers, and so on. In times of crisis especially, narrative's role in making the world meaningful is important. Literary studies can step in to provide sophisticated reading practices in response to students who often claim that what they learn has no bearing on their reality and that the knowledge taught does not address the urgency of climate change, Black Lives Matter, or other movements for justice.

In computing, a sandbox is a virtual space in which new or untested software or code can be run securely isolated from the rest of a network. For teachers of literature, story is such a sandbox because that is where a narrative can describe possible, probable, and actual social arrangements nevertheless distanced from reality. Note that there is a kind of paradox here that continues to engage the best literary theorists – it has to do with understanding the relationship (or non-relationship) between fiction and reality. Being distinct from reality means that story is a place where students of literature can safely imagine actions they or others might perform within specific fictional scenarios. It is also where readers get to engage with possible or probable outcomes. At the same time, this exercise of their imaginations could eventually become a rehearsal for real interventions to forestall or foster specific futures. Stories are where we imagine the kind of people we might have to become to really perform those actions. Thus, literacy plays a key role in preparing students for futures that are highly likely to differ radically from the past and present. In times of technological, material, and social change, it is important to give students the understanding to reflect on these cultures of change, and to provide the skills to effect change themselves.

One such way of learning to effect change is by bringing the body back into the classroom. The alienation spread by what Giroux calls "pandemic pedagogy" is accentuated in a virtual learning environment. However, it should by no means be taken for granted that face-to-face teaching automatically includes any practice of embodied learning. For that reason, I have been inspired by Louise Rosenblatt's focus on students' personal and performative involvement in reading as detailed in her seminal work *Literature as Exploration* (1938), later editions of which contain a "Coda" entitled "A Performing Art." Here, Rosenblatt (1966) refers to the worlds opened up in literary works, "we share, we participate in … we live in them," so much so that experience of a literary work is "a mode of living" (999–1000). Rosenblatt compares reading to the performance of a dance in which the reader's "own body" becomes "the formed substance that is the dance" (1000) because, she says, as teachers of literature "we are basically helping our students to learn to perform in response to a text" (279).

Rosenblatt's approach is in part a response to what she felt were shortcomings in the New Criticism insofar as this method tended to avoid "the historical and the social" in its instrumental focus on the apparatus of the text (1001). What I draw from her work is the emphasis on the reader's historically and socially situated capacity to creatively form her own experience of a text – including its aesthetic qualities – that then informs her perspective on the world. I see this as a fine balance of objectivity and subjectivity that does not renounce emotion as a means to precise readings that encompass reader, text, and social reality. This is explored in Case Study Two, "What the Coming-of-Age Novel Teaches Us About the Anthropocene." This case study includes discussions of J. D. Salinger's *The Catcher in the Rye*, Jacqueline Woodson's *Brown Girl Dreaming*, Toni Morrison's *Song of Solomon*, and Kazuo Ishiguro's *Never Let Me Go*. In this case study, I expand the terms with which we usually discuss the coming-of-age genre. While retaining the sense of an individual transition into adulthood, I suggest that such shifts toward maturity may also affect whole societies and even the human species. I point out that the genre often instructively thematises global environmental challenges that we as a species currently face. An important feature of this approach is that it runs counter to the sometimes extreme pessimism associated with our times. What emerges is a reading of the Anthropocene itself as a coming-of-age story that can mobilise hope rather than despair in the midst of crisis.

Coming of age, and crisis more generally, are times when many voices compete for attention and students can feel overwhelmed and distracted by this. I encourage them to vocalise their responses to literature as a means to help them develop agency they can express in a voice of their own. The experience of reading a book with ten, twenty people can be transformative: you not only read it with them but through their voices, their questions and interpretations, in a constant translation, a translation of the translation, from one language to the other, but also from one understanding to another. When you write a text with a group, negotiating every word, expanding the meaning, arguing, more nuances and subtleties emerge together with a sense of collective identification. Your voice starts to contain a multitude that does not drown you out.

A simple but effective exercise to assist students in expressing their views among others is *collaborative thinking and writing*. In groups of four or five, I ask participants to respond in writing to a set question or topic about the text they are currently studying. They share a sheet of paper they each take turns with. Once they are under way, as they pass the paper around, their task is to build on what the previous person has written. This means they should either add nuance to what is written on the paper in response to the question or, alternatively, they can reject what is written and state why. At the end of the round, they are left with a rough draft of a collaborative piece of writing. They can now either write a short paragraph based on what is written there or present it verbally. This exercise works equally well using a collaborative tool such as Google doc or even the chat function on Zoom with a single group of students. I like to do collaborative exercises such as this early in the term so as to create an optimal learning environment after first seeing how comfortable my students are with negotiating differences and engaging in critical writing.

Some of the exercises in the case studies of this book have been inspired by resonances with Kate Rigby's careful reading of the practice of "Contact Improvisation" as explored by Hellene Gronda.[3] Gronda refers to the body as both "a part of the physical world that can be acted upon, and the part of the physical world that enables me to act" (qtd in Rigby). Rigby's particular approach to Contact Improvisation emphasises its affirmation of the practitioner's uniquely physical place in the world whose "earth body" is profoundly joined to her own (45) since the earth, she declares, "is flesh of your flesh, bone of your bone" (46).

Together with this moment of consubstantiality with the physical world, Rigby also affirms "Earth itself" as having a separate existence as "the greater 'body' within which my small human one attains, temporarily, its own quasi-autonomous existence" (45). For Rigby, by familiarising ourselves with earth's "capacities and constraints, its tendencies and resistances, we become better attuned to where we are heading in our volatile corporeal interactions" (47). My hope for the collaborative and interactive exercises presented in this book is that they similarly affirm the agency of readers to embody their own unique readings of texts, including reading the world they live in, in ways that can enrich the world's life story.

Reading and writing communities often pre-exist the classroom or exist in addition to the classroom. As a matter of being resourceful, building on pre-existing communities seems more important than ever. This means overcoming the boundaries that often exist between academic and non-academic literary environments. In Case Study Three, "Things to Do With the Canon in the Classroom," I demonstrate activities inspired by the forms and methods of fan fiction that emphasise student engagement in co-producing new interpretations rather than consuming extant readings as in a transmission model of learning. Of interest here is the manner in which the canon endures not only because of qualities intrinsic to texts but also through the kind of attention generations of readers bring to them. I bring that level of critical engagement into the classroom and show teachers how these reading practices can be adapted to the contemporary classroom by looking at the fanfiction of Mark Twain's *Adventures of Huckleberry Finn*. I also explore how Bacigalupi's *Ship Breaker* renews or de-familiarises Charles Dickens' *Oliver Twist* regarding the role of child labour during the period of Industrialisation, as well as the significance of the nation-state and coal versus oil supplies. Finally, I read select passages from Melville's *Moby-Dick* for the insights they offer into navigating crisis. I also read the novel through the prism of recent solarpunk fiction to find correspondences between resource extraction and consumption with an appreciation of some of the affordances energy provides and that we cherish now similarly to the way we did in Melville's day.

Horizons of possibilities

The case studies in this book include theoretical frameworks, methods for interpretation and analysis, and practical hands-on activities to make the teaching of literature in the classroom more relevant and authentic in a world marked by crisis. I put old texts, and theories, in dialogue with new so that more adaptable reading methods can emerge that promote an awareness of literature's enduring relevance and its occasional prescience. As teachers of literature in times of crisis, one of our tasks is to revise the assumptions we as a learning community make about what is worth preserving and what we need to do differently. This is something our students must face as well in their own living situations and for both them and us it involves two kinds of thinking that Judith Langer outlines. One way to consider what to preserve and what to change is via Langer's distinction between "point-of-reference thinking" used to better understand and use existing knowledge and "horizons of possibilities" that we explore when we are breaking new ground and "are not sure where we are headed" (*Envisioning Knowledge* 32).

Langer's phrase "horizons of possibility" eschews the programmatic search for a defined goal in favour of a more imaginative engagement with the reality of times of uncertainty. In the literature class during times of crisis, students often discover that there is vastly more that is yet to be discovered – most of which is what we do not even know that we don't know. Langer calls this a "reconnaissance" (33) since there is much exploration that occurs without actually knowing the precise nature of the end goal. And yet the unknown also exists even among the life forms and their complex biology that are known to us. In short, there is a lot more going on than ordinary knowledge can account for. This is not to say that the more programmatic point-of-reference thinking is wrong but that, as Langer says, with the other method "the possibilities we can explore are open-ended" (32). Knowing when and why to deploy either of these approaches is important and it will come as no surprise that horizons of possibilities will be useful for developing in students a literacy to help discover new approaches to a world in flux.

Aspects of this form of thinking appear in Kagawa and Selby's advocacy of a tolerance for uncertainty and patience with errors in their discussion of how to address the calamity that climate change brings with it: "educational spaces should build a culture of learning awash with uncertainty and in which uncertainty provokes transformative yet precautionary commitment rather than paralysis" (243). Their language compellingly evokes images of flooding particularly attuned to our present time – it helps us to think of horizons that link the consequences of climate change to discovery without ignoring the seriousness of our predicament. And they recall and extend Reinertsen's "willingness to work with uncertainty" (4) referred to above. Important here is that, as well as improving students' literacy skills, reading literature with a readiness to explore horizons of possibilities is a way of learning how to read a world in crisis through appreciating complexity, living with uncertainty, and forgiving error. It is about questioning hegemony without dismissing systems thinking. Thus, while not dispensing with "point-of-reference thinking," it recommends an open-ended exploration rather than a hunt for predefined goals.

This is essentially a turning away from preconceptions that can be understood as relinquishing readings dependent on authorised knowledge and as such is consonant with Barthes' espousal of the death of the author. It also resonates with an area of Emanuel Levinas' thinking on language and liberation. I am also inspired by some of Levinas' statements on the emancipatory quality of saying as he distinguishes it from the said in *Otherwise than Being or Beyond Essence*. For Levinas, the notion of "other than being" refers to going beyond whatever is in its irreducible givenness or essence (1). It could be seen as a principle of creativity wherein saying is a productive gesture that exceeds the assumed fixed nature of the said. Paul Ricoeur helps us to appreciate this concept's bearing on literary studies facing crisis by according a political dimension to Levinas' more abstract argument seeing there an urgent call "to tear oneself away, through the otherwise than…, from the very thing whose reign one attempts to suspend or interrupt" (82, ellipsis in the original). Applying this to the teaching of literary practices, the said can be thought of as the object of analysis such as the text itself, or literature as a body of works. A student's response to that same text, on the other hand, is part of that text's saying. The saying is highly mobile and evolving, there for the student and teacher to discover as something genuinely new and emergent. It is important to realise that anything said can receive a different saying which, if it endures or is otherwise sustainable, takes on the status of a said.

Case Study Four, "Modern Again: Tell it from the Scars," explores further activities that empower student readers and writers to develop the "saying" of a text. In the same way that popular organisations such as the Zinn Education Project help teachers and students to think outside the box, my aim is to further break down the boundaries that still exist, despite advances in reader reception theory, between reading and writing – especially critical and creative writing – poetics and rhetorics, emotions and critique, theory and practice. Therefore, in this case study, I encourage the blurring of boundaries between high and popular culture. I demonstrate teaching strategies in which Henry James' *The Turn of the Screw* and T. S. Eliot's "The Waste Land" are read while overhearing Juliana Spahr's trenchant "Unnamed Dragonfly Species" and Elizabeth Acevedo's tour-de-force slam poetry in *The Poet X*, both of which reprise avant garde aesthetics and modernist themes. Coupled with that, I share with teachers the importance of seeing narrative at times as a testament of a crisis survived, as a form of marking or scar that signifies that a wound has healed. This is also as a way of informing students' creative writing endeavours with the potential to heal and develop resilience. Finally, the case study takes up the organic optimism of Federico Garcia Lorca's notion of *duende* as an inner force of creativity, authenticity, and renewal.

The image of a horizon of possibilities suggests a veritable geographical expansion of the scene of literary study, which I think is consistent with Langer's meaning. It concurs with Laura Dassow's declaration coming from her background as a scientific illustrator that "a book is less 'about' nature, a representation of it, than it 'is' nature, a participant in some larger ecology" (330). Dassow expands on a point made by Bruno Latour in *Politics of Nature* in which he affirms that language "is one of the material arrangements" by which the so-called objective world "grows": "reality grows to precisely the same extent as the work done to become sensitive to differences" (Latour qtd in Dassow). Dassow then asks in her exploration of what she calls deliberate reading, "How can literary studies become more sensitive to natural difference, 'grow' rather than suppress material 'reality'?" Thus, for her, turning attention to what in literature is "beyond representation," deliberate reading means "weighing the words one hears, against themselves, against the world, against the word of others" (331). As such, to read deliberately is a shift towards reading not for efficiency or fluency, but towards a spirit of play and invention.

Such a focus on the materiality of the reading process expands the horizon of possibilities in that it trains the student reader to become attuned to how a text's formal properties elicit sensations, feelings, and emotions, in addition to meaning. In order to develop this competence of processing both the emotional and the cognitive aspects of interpreting, I borrow from biologist Christopher Uhl's *four stages of reflection* from his book *Developing Ecological Consciousness: The End of Separation* (2003). When reflecting on a question, Uhl suggests that the student first offers their reactions by writing down quickly whatever comes to mind (step 1). Then, he suggests exploring these reactions by asking, "Why did I react that way to this question?" (step 2). Once this step is completed, students should be given a full 15 minutes to reflect and to persevere by taking it as far as possible (step 3). Finally, students should be asked to return to the same question, but now instead of answering from their head, Uhl instructs his students to "answer the question with your whole being … the point is to feel the question alive in you – and then simply be attentive to what feelings and thoughts arise in response" (27–28).

The question that comes up more often than any other when I teach my teacher-training students is, how to teach in a way that connects student to content and student to the world. As literature teachers in times of crisis we have a lot to learn from the other disciplines that train scientific observation of the natural world since this might just help to empower our students to use their reading skills as a way of engaging with the world. As a way of preparing for this engagement with the wider world, I recommend Uhl's questions provoking reflections that require confronting what is going on – inside a person and outside – and connecting the self with the wider world. These include questions such as "The universe is bathed in mystery … what are the mysteries in your life?" (27) or "Appearances aside, Earth is actually our larger body. Can you offer three personal examples to illustrate how this is literally true?" (53). This is only to serve as inspiration to come up with your own examples of reflection questions to enhance engagement with the world beyond representation.

Best practices for emergency remote teaching

For many teachers of literature, student participation exercises are an important part of an inspiring learning environment. During times of crisis, we can more consciously model conversations for how to respond to real-world challenges. Literary education needs to adapt, and quickly, to the rapidly changing conditions of our world. Beyond the enormous problem of climate change, we also face events such as the Black Lives Matter racial justice movement, economic and political disunity in the wake of Brexit and the lead-up to the 2020 US election, and the spring 2020 Covid-19 pandemic, and the list goes on. As teachers we now must learn to use new participation rubrics that acknowledge the trauma and grief of students. As well as this, we frequently need to answer doubts about the educational system and its value. At the same time, due to the pandemic, we are now teaching under radically different conditions from those of some few months ago. Now, many of us are teaching remotely or we are practising within a blended learning and teaching environment. For those who have been arguing for a more embodied pedagogy, the online classroom seems lacking in materiality and even humanity. Online teaching requires more from teachers who are now expected, in many cases, to bring something of the material world into the digital classroom when teaching a course that was not intended for online delivery. How do we combat loneliness and provide the conditions for sociality while offering online learning in times of crisis?

To begin with, Susan Ko's method of pacing is well worth adhering to. As she outlines it in her sample syllabus: "each class week begins on Monday and ends on Sunday" (123). Pacing the delivery of curriculum means that a seminar need not just be confined to a scheduled two-hour block which teachers and students attend at the same time and place. This could mean that a literature seminar begins with a *primer* or a conversation starter in the form of a provocative question or statement. Think of this as a simple real-world task or problem to solve. The responses can then be collected ahead of the actual class (via whatever platform you are using) to be discussed in class. This way of activating student interest prior to the conventional seminar time is certain to improve student engagement.

It's important to emphasise online learning taking the form of a community rather than a broadcast. This means we need to talk through the screen not at the screen. We do this by making sure that:

• The human is part of the online learning experience
• Dialogue remains part of the process of learning
• The material world is brought into the digital environment

For Sean Michael Morris, Zoom pedagogy is deficient in that it "puts full control of the classroom in the hands of the teacher, and almost entirely out of reach of students" ("Fostering Care and Community at a Distance"). In order to hand some of that control back to students, we first need to make sure they are confident to take it. Literature teachers know the value of establishing a caring, trusting environment to enable dialogue on matters that quite often have to do with growing up and the formation of subjectivity, embracing values, and expressing emotions. While some students struggle more than others to gain the confidence to speak openly with one another and their teacher in face-to-face classes or IRL (in real life), it is fair to say that it takes far more effort and time to achieve the same level of openness during an online seminar.

The communication that would happen organically following direct physical cues in a classroom now needs to be orchestrated and staged in advance by the teacher. For instance, the teacher can invite announcements or celebrations at the beginning of each class, or end-of-week summations to be posted as a chat. Students may be invited more regularly to give feedback about how a course is going for them and what we need to do for them to get the most out of the course. At the conclusion of a seminar, the teacher may invite students to say goodbye to each other as they would IRL. This can be done in a fun way by asking everyone to turn on their mikes and shout out their hellos or goodbyes simultaneously in the spirit of *a class chorus of voices*. Similarly, I invite students: *creatively introduce yourselves to each other*. They can use technology to their advantage, be it adding a selfie sticker to their favourite book cover, designing a personalised meme, using Google Maps to indicate a place in the world they would like to visit and why. The possibilities are endless.

Similarly, icebreaking exercises will likely take longer in the process of bringing a face-to-face course to an online delivery. I find virtual magnetic poetry a useful and at times moving exercise for students to do in order to both engage with literature as well as bring something of themselves onto the screen. Here is an exercise I recommend to my teacher-training students to enlist student participation. Using a random selection of words, *create a magnetic poem* online to engage with a teaching dilemma. A favourite of mine is: you have a student who is reluctant to read the assigned text. What would you say to that student using the random scramble of words offered on the screen?[4] Please bring your poem to class on Monday! Once in class, students show their poems and there is often quite a bit of laughter given the constraints. You may notice that (as typically) students tend to eschew using the entire online "magnetic board" and rather bunch up their stanza along the left-hand margin of the board. Here is an opportunity for them to learn more about the possibilities for freedom of poetic form if you encourage them to "own" that space and make it part of their expression.

An emergency situation like the 2020 pandemic necessitates going online at short notice and this puts an almost unbearable amount of pressure on the dedicated teacher who wishes for the classroom to continue to be a haven of normality in an otherwise chaotic world. Seldom is the process as seamless as we would like it to be. For many of us there are several hurdles that need to be negotiated. One of the most destructive aspects of crisis is that it tends to harm the social fabric of society and so, again, the act of modelling community is definitely the most important of all aspects of emergency remote teaching. This includes learning to engage with and monitor the online environment, maybe promoting the "post once, reply twice" rule on discussion forums, as well as making, wherever possible, personal contact with students. We can also model community by making a point of inviting colleagues and former students into the classroom as often as possible. Dialogue can also be maintained by breaking through the isolation via asynchronous teaching activities. For example, rather than doing annotations on their own, students can collaboratively generate conversation and ideas using online annotation tools such as hypothes.is, Perusals, Google Docs or other such file-sharing programs.

Learning can be greatly enhanced by finding ways to bring the material world into the digital. I sometimes ask students to list some objects in their room in the chat function of Zoom – five to seven things seems to be a good number. I then turn this into an instructive exercise about what constitutes narrative and what is required to *turn an itemised list into a story*. Once students have named and shared the names of the items, I devise a way of expanding each one so that it has a story attached to it. Asking for the reason why the thing stands out is often enough, but one could nuance that approach by prompting with, Who else do you know who knows about this object, and how did they come to that knowledge?

To conclude, a range of different crises often of a global scale is currently affecting students' emotional wellbeing and their ability and motivation to learn are often impacted as a result of these disruptions. Covid-19 has demonstrated the complexity of a crisis that is more than medical; it is also economic, environmental, and political. The global changes to education as a result of the crisis highlight the enormous challenges that a crisis poses to teachers, perhaps especially to those who teach in the humanities. After all, what use is reading in a world that's burning? In truth, reading practices are invaluable for framing and critically examining the challenges associated with crisis to help cope with grief and as a means to impart the skills needed to deal with crisis, such as adaptability, flexibility, resilience, and resistance. In times of cultural and socio-economic change, it is important to give students a chance to reflect on events and to provide them with the skills to effect change themselves rather than succumb to frustration and despair. This is best achieved through collaborative competency that aims to overcome fear and suspicion by fostering dialogue and cooperation with others.

Notes

1 The pursuit of safety especially in education has been critiqued by Jonathan Haidt and Greg Lukiano in *The Coddling of the American Mind* (2018) in which they refer to it as "safetyism."
2 Cathy Davidson reminds us that "Professionalism in higher education became almost synonymous with specialization, in sharp contrast to earlier historical ideals of what it meant to be a learned individual, such as the 'Renaissance man,' a multitalented, versatile, visionary, cross-disciplinary thinker" (38–39).
3 Rigby notes that Contact Improvisation was originated by Steve Paxton in 1970s New York.
4 For example, http://play.magneticpoetry.com/poem/Original/kit/

1

CASE STUDY ONE

Discovering the weird and the wonderful in a changing world

Texts: *Alice's Adventures in Wonderland; Parable of the Sower; Southern Reach* **trilogy**

In this case study I bring Lewis Carroll's *Alice in Wonderland* into proximity with Octavia E. Butler's speculative fiction, *Parable of the Sower* and New Weird author Jeff VanderMeer's *Southern Reach* trilogy. Though the works span more than 150 years, they offer didactic opportunities to speak to a post-anthropocentric age. They question hegemony and normativity, they encourage critique and systems thinking through the adaptation of myth and storytelling, they also confront rational thought with alternative logics. In this case study, I show how literary analysis can further an appreciation of complexity – "staying with the trouble" (Haraway). Specifically, I show through student participation techniques, collaborative reading, and writing, how literacy, including critical and creative thinking, plays an important role in improving knowledge about how to adapt to new challenges. Literacy, broadly speaking, and sophisticated reading practices are integral to the development of the reading skills needed in a classroom that can adapt to a rapidly changing environment. This method of reading creates a fluctuating and flexible space for closely reading texts in dialogue with one another and the world of the reader. As will be seen, I read these texts as quest narratives not necessarily to define them as such but rather in order to affirm to student readers in times of crisis that they can see themselves as embarked on a quest and that their reading is part of this.

Alice's Adventures in Wonderland

Lewis Carroll's well-known children's fantasy begins during a time of leisurely boredom for Alice that is soon interrupted by the first of a series of very strange encounters. While sitting with her sister on a riverbank, wondering if it is worth her while getting up to collect daisies for a daisy chain, Alice sees a rather anxious White Rabbit hurrying off to goodness knows where. Without a moment's hesitation, Alice follows him into a rabbit-hole. What happens next concurs with the experience of many people during an accident or other emergency when the passage of time seems to slow down. Almost immediately, Alice is falling vertically down a deep well and yet this takes place in such slow motion that she can observe with curiosity the sights she sees as she descends while also reflecting on several other matters as well. She tries to apply the geography she has learnt at school to determine if she might fall right through the earth. It is significant for this case study that, although Alice wonders what her present latitude or longitude is, she "had not the slightest idea what Latitude was, or Longitude either" (5).

Even in the early stage of her adventures – crises marked by curiosity or wonder more than anxiety – Alice's lack of accurate bearings means she applies the principle of heading for the open-ended spaces of the unknown. In this, she employs Langer's principle of "horizons of possibility" rather than simply building on what she knows. Her quest, so to speak, is for what she has little inkling of. Also of interest for us, Alice soon discovers that throughout her adventures she will need to adapt her scale or stature to fit into the situations she wishes to explore, the means to do so always fortuitously appearing when needed. This is a reminder that one cannot expect to endure the passage through a crisis without undergoing significant changes in oneself. This feature of crisis becomes evident soon after Alice begins to explore the strange world around her when she reaches a double impasse. First, she enters a hall full of locked doors and a tiny key that fits none of them and then she notices a tiny door that will open but that she cannot fit through. She knows she needs to be smaller but has no idea how to become so (8–9). A feature of the bizarre situations that confront her is that they awaken in her a belief in unheard-of capabilities – such as shrinking and growing so as to be able to fully enter into the world she discovers down the rabbit-hole.

Alice's Adventures in Wonderland provokes questions to do with scale and knowledge or, more precisely, how to chart a course for the unknown. A crisis can make us feel bewilderingly small or, for that matter, disconcertingly large, even though our actual size remains the same – and it can render everything we think we know rather insignificant in the light of the changes it brings. I was once in conversation with a colleague about the #MeToo movement and we concluded that the recognition gained by it has made us, as female, middle-aged scholars feel vindicated, a little taller and stronger, more capable of entering into a new stage of debate on and activism for women's rights. Conversely, so many aspects of the climate change crisis make many people feel small and powerless. However, Alice's adventures teach us that strange new events do not happen independently of us as observers – they bring with them reasons and pressure for us to adapt, either for or against.

Recent years have been about both growing and shrinking, and not only in ourselves but also in the scale of our endeavours. In times of crisis, there is probably no point in aiming for that familiar "aha-moment" when the teacher dazzles the students by revealing a particular interpretation of a passage or a stanza as if the text encodes a deep secret and the teacher is an oracle. When exploring the unknown, such moments do not ring true since the idea of a singular reading, no matter how brilliant, narrows the field of possibilities too much. While being a valid method in itself, it is unnecessarily goal-oriented, like decoding a treasure map to find where X marks the spot where the booty is buried. A crisis does not contain a solution that someone has hidden beforehand. Rather, there may be many solutions, and many that can work together with others. Finding them requires imagination to work with what is at hand often while putting it to unfamiliar uses. To take an example, in conversation with the Cheshire Cat, when Alice declares, "I don't want to go among mad people," it is tempting to read the exchange that follows as a simple indictment of the human species as a whole:

> "Oh, you can't help that," said the Cat: "we're all mad here. I'm mad. You're mad."
> "How do you know I'm mad?" said Alice.
> "You must be," said the Cat, "or you wouldn't have come here."
>
> *(90)*

An eco-critical response to this passage would likely conclude that we must be mad since it "raises the question of whether a rational species would choose to get to the point where it is addicted to growth, consumption and other patterns of thinking and action that ultimately threaten its very own existence" (Milne et al. 802–803). I wonder, how helpful is such an observation in a crisis situation? However insightful this reading may be, it keeps to the already known binary of sane–mad to advance a proposition that is hardly controversial and not nearly playful enough.

By reading the Cheshire Cat's remark straightforwardly as above, the unsurprising take-home message is that you, the student or reader, are mad because you are part of the problem. However, to develop resilience and resourcefulness in students during times of upheaval, we often need to eschew the overly familiar and invite further complexity on a much broader scale. In contrast to making a familiar critique of the human, one could look for something that is more of a provocation, a response to the Cheshire Cat that is more likely to offer the student the encouragement to find a range of alternative paths in place of a simple right-or-wrong fork in the road. Apart from that, the untroubled and playful tone of Lewis Carroll's story reminds me that to be able to conduct teaching at all in times of crisis might seem to beg the question, What crisis? I mean, if there are classes being run, and texts (admittedly, some rather sombre ones too, not just *Alice's Adventures*) and above all *time* to engage in the study of literature, then surely at least those of us involved in such pursuits are not actually facing a crisis. Well, to get a strongly worded answer to that question I could just ask some of my students.

As I have mentioned, a feature of our times is that students often themselves raise serious doubts as to the relevance of literary studies, or any schooling at all – the school strikes for the climate have taught us this. But to address the fact that the relative calm of a seminar room seems to belie a state of crisis, we need only recollect the lessons taught by Timothy Morton and Rob Nixon. They both refer to global calamities that exist presently and affect every person on earth now and for generations to come but, either because of their vast spatial distribution ("hyperobject") or the glacial slowness of their onset ("slow violence"), they are almost impossible for most of us to see. And there are crises that should be there for all to see, such as racism and injustice, but that nevertheless are overlooked in public discourse until movements like #MeToo and Black Lives Matter bring them more starkly into view.

There is a strong case to be made for the value of literary studies to be taught during crises and it has to do with how storytelling cannot be silenced by crisis and nor can stories be erased. On the contrary, in times of turmoil there are more stories not fewer, and the one thing they all have in common is that they insist on being heard and for this they demand that we take the time to attend to them. To put it in Alice-in-Wonderland terms: instead of falling headlong down the bottomless well of a crisis, to take heed of stories and seek out their counsel is actively to slow down our response to crisis rather than feed its flames.

The playfulness of *Alice's Adventures in Wonderland* allows me to be comfortable with a degree of confusion as to what it might all mean, and this frees me to embark on a joint adventure with my students. The novel ludicrously juxtaposes the imperious Queen of Hearts and her terrified courtiers with Alice and other subversives (such as the Cheshire Cat) and is thus a light-hearted text dealing with how to sidestep real anxiety. Like Alice, I am mostly ignorant of the forces that cause a crisis to break out, yet I too follow a trail that seems relevant to me, even though I do not know from the outset fully how it is relevant. I glimpse what I don't quite know rushing past me like a White Rabbit anxiously announcing how late it is. For whom is time short? For what might it be running out? Readings vary depending on what one makes of the Rabbit. Before rushing to any conclusion, I want to investigate the matter with my students. I apply some pacing to the Lewis Carroll seminar by setting up a *primer* for students ahead of a shared discussion, portioning out the seminar time to include this pre-seminar activity. For the primer I post this question for them to mull over:

> "Imagine noticing #OhdearOhdearIshallbelate starting to trend on some of your feeds. Before you investigate online, you think about what it might refer to. What do you come up with?"

They are invited to record their answers in words/image/sound on a Padlet page simply accessed via phone or computer and immediately shared with the rest of the class. During the days before the seminar, I'm delighted when someone posts, "I never feel there is enough time any more – how can we slow down?" I respond by pointing out that the opening pages of *Alice's Adventures* deal with speed and slowness and suggest that the group do a close reading looking for what can be learned from Alice's slow-motion fall.

Questions emerge from student discussions. I offer questions as well. What is important is that a resourceful way to think about crisis is that it can be imbued with a spirit of quest. And let's not forget that quest is at the root of the word question and questions are usually more important than answers when tackling the unknown. Is there some part of nature that feels time is short? Does Alice feel it? What does the speed of life have to do with power structures? These reflections become a way of linking learning about literature to our experience of the world and to get an increased understanding of how the two are entwined, or even networked. I take the students through the point I made just now about how stories insist that we slow down enough to focus on them. What do we fill the time with when this happens? I get some responses: critical thinking, pleasure of being entertained. Not everyone in the class is highly vocal so I'm pleased when some time after the face-to-face session ends I see the Padlet still receiving further responses to this.

In order to explore the quest motif in literature, I introduce students to the *compare the quest* activity in which I present them with a list of standard features of quest narrative so that they can assess any possibly quest-like characteristics of the text we are studying. You can compile your own list; I have adapted mine from one supplied by Jenny Grahame and Kate Oliver in their teaching compendium for Suzanne Collins' *The Hunger Games*. In their exercise, they instruct students to note down how the quest motif is treated in that novel. The following are among the features of the quest narrative that are particularly pertinent to crisis, especially because they underscore both the challenges and rewards of change:

- A problem forces the hero (usually male) to set off on a journey with a specific goal
- The goal is a reward or a prize, often a magical object. This can be something new, or it can be something that was stolen from the hero
- The hero enters an extraordinary world, a land of adventures, tests and magical awards
- The hero brings back the prize or reward

(Grahame and Oliver 15)

Students may post reflections in a shared Google Doc or any other collaborative tool. Unsurprisingly, someone notes that Alice is female, though this does not much resemble a feminist tale and she does not have a specific goal. I point out that the absence of a goal might align the story more with an open-ended quest. We discuss this possibility – that one might be in quest for something one knows not what. Apart from that, there is general agreement that Alice seems to be on a quest because she enters a land of adventures. However, the story doesn't seem to contain a clearly defined prize or reward that Alice brings back with her. Add to this the fact that the "problem" at the start of Alice's adventures is merely boredom, which is not a very heroic spur to action. It occurs to me then that an often-discussed stage of crisis is when the public lose interest in it because they have been overwhelmed with stories about the problem. Boredom within a seemingly interminable crisis is itself a separate problem and – without needing to imagine what Alice's initial crisis might have been – it is possible to review her adventures as perfectly suited to dealing with this second-order crisis.

While their findings may indicate that the quest motif as a literary theme is less pertinent for reading *Alice's Adventures in Wonderland*, the quest as a methodology is even more useful. One example of learning from the quest motif is found in the chapter "Advice from a Caterpillar" (59) and it is most suitable for close reading. Once again, size is at the heart of the conundrum here as the hookah-smoking caterpillar informs Alice that one side of the mushroom he is sitting on "will make you grow taller, and the other side will make you grow shorter" (68). The only problem is that a mushroom being circular has no sides and, even if it did, Alice is not told which produces what effect. This lack of coordinates for reading the world recalls Alice's earlier ignorance of latitude and longitude. This precipitates Alice's courageous and arbitrary first step into the unknown followed by her undertaking a scientific investigation by which she samples both sides of the mushroom until she is satisfied that she shrinks when eating from her right hand and grows from her left hand. Her quest, in other words, was for a useful method of adapting to her surrounds and soon we hear Alice declare she has "got back to my right size" (74).

A few sentences more and the chapter concludes with Alice discovering a "four feet high" house that she believes will take her to "that beautiful garden" and thus she "began nibbling at the right-hand bit again, and did not venture to go near the house till she had brought herself down to nine inches high" (75). Students can be challenged further at this point. How does she know that she has reached the right size? Is there such a state as being the "correct" size (or one correct approach) especially during times of crisis? Instead, circumstances demand that one adapts to each encounter. The quest methodology provokes an ongoing inquiry that does not have a halting point. And it emerges that one of the awards that comes from the quest is the fact of Alice's having proven that she is up to the problems encountered through her demonstrated resilience and ability to adapt. In a crisis, knowledge sometimes matters less than knowing how to comport oneself. If an unknown remains an unknown we have nevertheless developed ways of dealing with it. Thus readers of the quest methodology in Alice will develop a tolerance of error and understand the value of forgiveness. This also has a lot to do with embracing the principle of change, as seen in the next novel. Change is sometimes felt to be a problem whereas upsetting of the status quo is inevitable and not necessarily negative.

Parable of the Sower

Octavia Butler's *Parable of the Sower* (2000[1993]) is more obviously about a girl on a quest, albeit in circumstances more catastrophic than Alice's. Set in the 2020s of a fictional but plausible twenty-first century, the novel's world has been severely damaged by climate change and the ruthless exploitation of natural resources. A young African-American woman named Lauren Oya Olamina has grown up in a gated community on the outskirts of Los Angeles. Lauren hits on an unusual strategy for survival. In a time when radical unexpected change is the only permanent feature of existence, rather than defy it she subtly *deifies* crisis by proposing a "God-is-change belief system" (135). This is the central tenet of her belief and a new religion which she calls Earthseed. According to her insights, Lauren affirms that humankind is not necessarily the subject or victim of God as change. To embrace this deep truth about the way things are is to become an adaptable agent of God who can invite radical change rather than resisting it. Lauren is a writer, author of her own scripture in verses that recur in the novel, such as

> *All that you touch,*
> *You change.*
> *All that you change,*
> *Changes you.*
>   *(138, emphasis in*
>   *the original)*

She is also an educator, or she will be once she has collected all her verses into an exercise book for people to read, "to pry them loose from the rotting past" (139). In this novel, it is possible for the endless potential of human resourcefulness and the inherent will to adapt and survive to reach a harmony with an endlessly changing universe. But even with these insights, for Lauren the pace of change is also a challenge and her aim to use her wisdom to teach others will come to fruition, perhaps, "if everything will just hold together for just a few more years" (139).

Lauren gathers a group of survivors and sets out to form a new community in which people will live according to the teachings of Earthseed, a practice that involves planting seeds and finding new stories to tell. *Parable of the Sower* thematises the making of an alternative, more sustainable economy in the shadow of a crumbling, petroleum-fuelled American Dream. A big part of that social reconstruction is via Lauren's writing. In the novel, this is where important meanings are generated and negotiated, policies thought through and envisioned, and politics analysed and possibly even practised. In light of this, the intended learning outcomes for reading Butler's novel include the ability to:

- Identify narrative relationships between the private and public, micro- and macro-politics
- Discover new models for economic wellbeing and social justice based on acknowledged limits to growth
- Explore the power of narrative in shaping the future by first imagining it

My aim is to mobilise pedagogical methods in support of the above outcomes as they emerge from one of the novel's own key concerns of teaching through writing. I look for exercises that foster an appreciation of the purposes of teaching literature as well as the creative and imaginative processes that bring it into existence. The learning activities I have in mind for this unit are those that test *Gestaltungskompetenz*, which focuses on action and literally means "shaping competence" or "design ability" though the term has more specific meanings. Some of these are drawn from commentaries on the UN Decade of Education for Sustainable Development (ESD) and it is no surprise that they are directly relevant to crisis. For example, one paper's abstract refers to "specific skills and capabilities needed to decide and act in situations of uncertainty and complexity."[1] The following activity during reading is useful for enabling a purposeful treatment of narrative as a resource for sustainable design – we could even think of it a literary "upcycling," extracting parts of a text that can be used for other things. This engages students in a reading process that at the same time produces further written works based on one text – they are literally making something new from a literary work:

Poetry scrapbook: Ask your students to select 15–20 sentences or fragments of sentences from the novel. There is no need for any defined criteria for selection – that may or may not become clear later. At the outset, students need only choose from sentences that grab their attention. Preferably, the sentence fragments should come from several or all chapters rather than just one place. Students should bring their list to the virtual or face-to-face seminar. During the seminar they are given a few minutes to select seven to ten samples from their sets. When time is up, instruct the students to design a poem based on what remains of the list. They are not allowed to add any words, but they can change the order in which they appear. Students are then invited to call on each other to read their poems aloud and to comment on them. Students are usually very comfortable sharing poems made in this way since they comprise someone else's words. Since they choose words and fragments based on their initial emotional impact, the result often yields for each of them a surprisingly personal access to the novel beyond the more obvious thematics. The poems can be collated in a shareable document and shared with the class as a memento of the seminar. The following are examples.

Student #1	Student #2	Student #3
I see the sudden	The few stars we could see	God can't be resisted or
light streak of	were	stopped, but
a meteor	windows into heaven	can be shaped and focused.
flashing westward	Is any of this real?	I feel what I see others feeling
across the sky	I felt it die, and yet I had not	a big-daddy-God or a
the stars are	died	big-cop-God
free	No, I think your world is	or a big-king-God
I can take	coming to	twenty-five or thirty lumpy,
a lot of pain	an end, and maybe you with	incoherent rewrites
without	it	he's good at reading me
falling apart	Destiny of Earthseed is to	Become a partner of God
as far as I'm concerned	take root	I found the name, found it
space exploration	among the stars	while I was weeding
can help us	From its own ashes	I'll have to do something
more than hurt us	A phoenix	about it
	First	Try to hide in all the work
	Must	there is to do
	Burn.	

This exercise can stand by itself as a purely practical way to promote the pleasure of creatively responding to a text. What requires a separate discussion is the matter of how this relates to less obvious forms of sustainability. For that, after the exercise, it is helpful to contextualise the process by starting a discussion exploring sustainability in literary studies. As usual, this can also be started with a primer question that sparks interest prior to the next seminar. Regardless of how the lesson is paced, I start with simple questions. What do we mean by sustainability? What is sustainability in literature? So far, the responses might be unsurprising – familiar matters like recycling, decreased consumption, wasting less, and so on come up and all these activities can be referenced in fiction. There is of course no harm in the thematisation in literature of pressing social concerns like resource scarcity or environmental degradation, I look at this below, but I'm also interested in testing if literary studies can involve us in an awareness shift that touches more deeply on these matters. I then ask the class, in relation to sustainability, what they think about the *poetry scrapbook* exercise. How might writing and reading be more or less sustainable? Is there a wasteful way to write, or a consumerist way to read? Do literary studies use energy? How are they paid for and by whom?

A good focus for class discussion is the nature of boundaries and the binary distinctions these often define. A thematic boundary that runs through the novel is, on one hand, Lauren's extreme openness to others – her at times debilitating empathy – and, on the other, the power of an impenetrable wall to exclude others such as the one guarding Oliver, Lauren's gated community. Direct your students' attention to the first three short chapters that describe the city of Oliver, owned by an energy company and trapped between the rising sea on one side and the desperation of the have-nots on the other. At the beginning of the novel, Lauren remembers a prophetic dream in which she recognises that the wall that is intended to protect the neighbourhood from "poor-squatters, winos, junkies, and homeless people in general" (23) is actually "a crouching animal, perhaps about to spring, more threatening than protective" (14). The capacity to interrogate fundamental aspects of the conceptual apparatus commonly used to make sense of the world – such as walls or defining lines – is important and the aim is not always to jettison distinctions. In what ways might a static, concrete wall embody the agency and threat of a dangerous animal? What sort of boundaries (ones that define binary distinctions or other things) are necessary? Which ones might be harmful? Lauren's powerful foreboding bears directly on the forces that seek permanently to define her world – forces that manifest in a wall – which is at the same time something at odds with her reality in which radical change is inexorable. Lauren is up against powerful forces and I wonder if the novel satisfies many or any of the criteria of a quest narrative. It is often helpful to run the *compare the quest* activity again, not to prove the point one way or another but to focus on the text with a new analytical lens.

Another productive focus in this novel that can be applied to others is to identify the ways in which thinking structures are represented. I ask how these pose a challenge to characters in the novel or, beyond it, to readers dealing with real-life versions of these structures. For example, through seminar discussions we analyse the way resources are depicted. The desalination plant that turns salt water into drinking water with solar power is a valuable asset for the city. This asset must, however, be sold off in exchange for protection from the many poor who desperately seek to gain access to that supply of water. A binary set of conflicting needs emerges quite clearly and we can then look at Lauren's teachings or other aspects of the novel for clues about how to deal with this apparent impasse. I point out that it is the kind of conflict that routinely shows up in discussions of how best to protect the environment and to safeguard economic stability as well. Could Lauren's religion of God as change working through human agency advise on such matters?

A perhaps less obvious binary is the role of Lauren's storytelling as a way to relate and connect to others in unexpected ways versus the nomadic migration of the Earthseed community and other refugees heading away from close contact with the parent community as they become a stateless, borderless band of out-siders on the outside of all enclosures. We note that there exists in Butler's *Parable of the Sower* a narrative that counters competitive social configurations with new intimate clusters and communities. At the close of the novel, Lauren and her group take on the task of forming a community detached from the practicalities and the imaginaries of modern capitalism through a return to a basic way of surviving in the here and now. Automation and large-scale production give way to small-scale endeavours: "Everything will have to be done by hand – composting, watering, weeding, picking worms or slugs or whatever off the crops and killing them one by one if that's what it takes" (560). In this way Butler's novel offers guidance to those who are torn by a conflict in which they need to belong to a community and yet they wish to distance themselves from many of that community's values or actions.

Although students in discussions can refer to action and even activism, and though they use concrete imagery and the language of feeling and emotion to persuade and rebut, it is it not at first easy for beginners to enter into discourse in a full-blooded way that enables them, for example, fully to feel the force of an argument and counter-argument. This is not surprising since a lot of the traditional activities of literary studies are quite cerebral, engaging the rational mind or the imagination rather than the body. This is why it is easier to photograph dance or a football game or a protest march than people engaged in study. As an activity it appears to be doing very little. For this reason, I look for bridging activities that can subtly lend a more muscular weight to the impressions mobilised by reading and writing. This is especially important when literary study is addressed to students with a view to giving them insights they can act on to affect the future they will take on. Apart from anything else, this is a way students learn to be attentive to the nuances of narrative and how these form the basis of action based on conviction and commitment to the future.

Not all narrative is a spur to action – stories and the discourses in which they arise and circulate can also seem to have a paralysing effect. During times of crisis, the sound of doom and gloom and the shrill sounds of warning tend to make us less tuned in to the possibilities for opportunity and potential for renewal and growth, less able to believe in purposeful engagement with the world. Although this may not be a problem for everyone, research suggests that there is a polarisation of the young who are either optimistic about the future or severely negative (see for example Ojala and Rubin). I don't suggest that there are simply right or wrong discourses and that one must always be engaged in specific action with "positive" goals. On the contrary, times of social upheaval do not furnish readers with certainties despite the claims of some ideologues. I insist that, like Alice in Wonderland and Lauren in her dystopian America, it is important to maintain an open-minded willingness to explore and a faith in one's capacity to read the world and even – in Lauren's case – to write out a new rule book.

To get in touch with the physicality of reading, and to counter the immobilising power of fearful discourse, I suggest engaging with texts in a way that uses more of the body. Examples of this are reading passages aloud and *situated reading* that aims to feel the impact of a text by reading it in different environments. This is followed by noting the changes and insights these various processes bring to the content on the page. I'm looking for a reading that can listen for subtle or dramatic shifts in significance through attention to one's own body as a register of the affects brought about by the text, sometimes read in a specific place. I believe this can sensitise readers to the affective nature of what they read. Moreover, knowing how to bring about and modulate their own affective responses through situated reading means students learn to be aware of and even defend themselves against the powerful influence of the media as it addresses them with public discourses coming from a wide range of interest groups.

When teaching online, it is even more important to bring the physicality of reading into the learning environment, and the activity *training your ear* can be practised without much effort. Here's how you could instruct the students on what to do: Choose a passage full of emotional variety and proceed to read it out loud to yourself, or to another person. How did reading the passage aloud affect your sense of the passage? Did it reinforce your initial interpretation or prompt a revision? What about your sense of the text as a whole? Return to your selected passage. Now annotate how you would read it after having reflected on the questions above. Where will your emphasis fall? Will you read it loudly, quietly, angrily, softly, choppily, smoothly, joyfully, sensually? When you then meet with your students, face-to-face or online, take the opportunity to look at the kinds of engagement formed between student and text. Perhaps some of your students are willing to instruct someone else in a performance of their chosen passage. This would allow the group as a whole to reflect on how individual attention to words and sentences affects the collective reception of a text. It is important here for students to understand that in being affected by what they read they are shaping and being shaped by the text. This recalls Lauren's dictum, *All that you touch, You change. All that you change, Changes you.*

Southern Reach trilogy

In this section I come at the idea of the porosity of borders and encourage students to encounter and explore the interface between the human and non-human. This might involve teaching the student that what is often understood as Other and described objectively is in actual fact not completely separate from the student; the two may even mutually define aspects of each other. According to some educators, pedagogical approaches that are informed by this principle of the porosity of defining boundaries are a good basis for the future viability of the humanities in higher education (Siddiqui). I present students with a *Tree of Life* diagram (Figure 1.1). There is a range of versions of this diagram, which graphically represents the vast field of known life forms within which the human is a very tiny subset. I point out that this is contained within an estimated even larger field of the life forms still unknown to science. Contemplating such a diagram is a useful conversation starter for any class on nature writing, or in which Anthropocentric themes in literature are discussed, or any class in which any human struggle is in focus. Its use lies in illustrating the enormous difference in scale between the finite set of what is visible, familiar, or comprehensible, on one hand, and, on the other, the incalculable extent of what is not known.

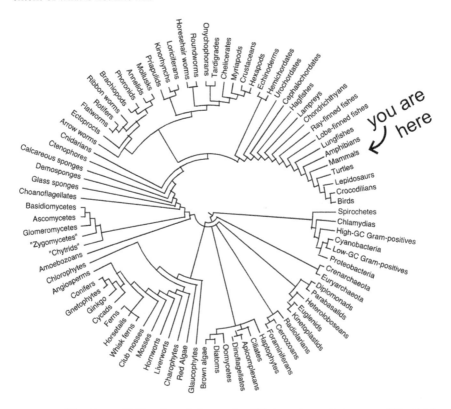

FIGURE 1.1 The Tree of Life, adapted from a simplified version at *Laboratory of David M. Hillis* based on a figure in the Appendix to *Life: The Science of Biology*, 9th ed., by D. Sadava, D. M. Hillis, H. C. Heller, and M. Berenbaum (Sinauer Associates and W. H. Freeman, 2011).

There is an abundance of life that is not human, although a lot of its DNA is contained within the human genome. It is against this background that we can understand the value of what might seem to be aimless or exploratory thinking since this is oriented towards the vast unknown rather than predicated on pre-existing knowledge. In New Weird author Jeff VanderMeer's *Southern Reach* trilogy (*Annihilation, Authority*, and *Acceptance*, all published in 2014), there are many encounters with non-human life. More precisely, the trilogy examines in intimate detail the sensations and significance of non-human, probably alien, life metabolising within the human since, in the trilogy, whatever border we imagine separating the human from its Other has always already been breached.

VanderMeer has announced in an interview that the stories were provoked by the massive oil spill following an explosion on the Deepwater Horizon oil platform in the Gulf of Mexico on 20 April 2010. It was to become the worst industrial accident in US history. Initially, VanderMeer's response to the tragedy was to speculate on the transgressive nature of oil and he describes a strange dream in which the oil never stopped leaking, a dream that became an inspiration for the novels. Moreover, he points out that by enduring in minute traces in the environment, its consequences are in fact potentially endless. "After the oil spill," VanderMeer notes, "I knew that at the microscopic level the oil was still infiltrating and contaminating the environment. That just because you can't see something doesn't mean it isn't affecting you or the places you love" ("A Writer's Surreal Journey").

For our purpose, it is essential to see that here the human has brought a crisis to the non-human – the animal and vegetable life that forms the Gulf ecology. At the same time, the crisis for that environment is also one for the human and not just those who depend for their livelihoods on the abundant life of the Gulf fisheries. When the distinction between the human and non-human is troubled, everyone is involved. And so we can see that although boundaries help us to define features of the world and understand their relationships, part of that understanding is that the boundaries are often porous and even arbitrary. When thinking about crisis, it can help to acknowledge its wider impacts and those of our responses so that we do not inadvertently hit on short-term solutions that have worse long-term impacts beyond our immediate human scope.

In VanderMeer's trilogy, the eponymous Southern Reach is an organisation set up to investigate a perilous region that appeared somewhere on a remote part of the Florida coast some decades before the story begins. Here, life forms and physical laws morph inexplicably resulting in bizarre experiences and producing mutations with often horrific consequences for those who pass its enigmatic and invisible border. Despite the hazards, Southern Reach has sent many expeditionary teams in to learn about this place that comes to be known as Area X and it turns out that, despite appearances, few if any have ever returned. The first novel, *Annihilation*, details the most recent expedition by an all-female group and is told from the perspective of the team's biologist whose experience of Area X becomes the key focus for readers.

I want to focus on something that comes up a number of times in the novels. We are reminded of the border-crossing potential of writing in which the material properties of text have the power to penetrate and physically affect a reader from the inside – in fact, the distinction between the inside and the outside becomes unstable. An early feature of the biologist's perspective is that her own body comes under the influence of Area X through proximity to an unusually "influential" form of writing. Initially, while reading from this strange, moss-like outgrowth on a wall, the biologist feels that the meaning of the mysterious words it forms is affecting her, "already those initial phrases were infiltrating my mind in unexpected ways, finding fertile ground" (24). The horticultural metaphor suggests that words and their meanings could behave like seeds or simply take root. Soon the biologist inhales actual spores from the living lettering and begins to display unusual physical symptoms she comes to call "the brightness," which affects her with a marked empathy towards Area X though it does not diminish her scientific interest. Key to the significance of this often-recalled phenomenon of the writing growing on the wall is the suggestion that it communicates not via the words but by altering the biology of those who come in contact with it.

VanderMeer's biologist is not simply the subject of the transformative influence emanating from the living text she is exposed to. She is in many ways an ecological hero profoundly responsive to the environmental crises of our times. She recalls the sometimes debilitating empathy of Butler's Lauren in *Parable of the Sower* by embodying an acute – and increasingly so – capacity to *feel with* the environments she studies. "My sole gift or talent, I believe now," she recalls, "was that places could impress themselves upon me, and I could become a part of them with ease" (*Annihilation* 108). She also manages to retain her sense of scientific objectivity in precise observations of the changes she undergoes, thus she retains the professional interest of a scientist but also seems to see herself increasingly as open to material and agential influences from the environment she is studying. "The wind was like something alive," she remarks, "it entered every pore of me" (74).

It is soon clear that the biologist is becoming other than the person she was and is taking on new qualities due to her physical contact with biological matter from Area X. Eventually, her scientific objectivity seems to be coupled with an alien perspective that may be studying her as much, or more than, she is studying it. "I did not feel as if I were a person but simply a receiving station for a series of overwhelming transmissions" (179). I focus on moments in fiction such as these that model an understanding of how humans discover the extent to which they themselves are intimately enmeshed in the web of life, particularly during times of crisis. Indeed, such a discovery can itself be understood as a crisis that shatters conventional definitions of self and other. VanderMeer's *Annihilation* lends an increased embodied awareness of one's physical presence as part of multiple, colliding assemblages with numerous intersecting boundaries. There is typically a big focus on individual writing assignments in the literature classroom. VanderMeer's novel encourages a different kind of teaching and learning environment in which individual writing assignments are interspersed with *collaborative journaling*. If teaching online, then it is relatively easy to include a shared Google doc or a Padlet in which students can contribute anonymously to a shared journal on a given topic. Bernadette Mayer, poet and visual artist associated with the Language Poets and the New York School, has a list of fantastic journal ideas that is publicly available.[2]

These novels offer many thought experiments on the fluid nature of boundaries that can ultimately lead students to understand that they can play an active role in defining the world they will live in. While keeping in mind that that world has a separate existence which shapes them, they get to see that they too can, to some extent, be shapers of their world as active parts of something larger than themselves. This last point is a fundamental principle of how learning works, according to Wiggins and McTighe (*Examining* 27). This also includes students' reading and responding as part of a larger environmental imaginary in which they can find localised perspectives of their own on crisis even though it may be very widespread. For a practical exercise in how this is done I aim to teach them how to express strong personal feeling that draws expressive power from the world around them. This will become a tool for sharing the strong emotions they often feel during times of crisis that can grow into an empowering capability to use language to enlist the support of others in creating alternatives.

I thus end this chapter with a focus on a writing exercise that I call *a tale twice told*. It develops the skills and competences I refer to above and, at the same time, gives teachers a window into the tremendous agitation and sometimes despair felt by their students. As teachers of literature in times of crisis, we do not want to discourage students from incorporating strong feelings into their works as this is an important outlet of emotion. However, we do want to help our students transfer the impact of strong personal feelings into something that can be shared with others. It is this aspect of their writing that usually constitutes a possible area of improvement rather than the use of feelings per se. The intended learning outcomes for this activity therefore include the ability to:

- Develop a concrete language for stories students care about
- Convey emotion using language that moves readers
- Maintain objectivity while dealing with strong feelings

In the first part of the exercise, students are instructed to describe the physical appearance of something they can presently see and maybe even touch, be it a vase of flowers or a smudge on the wall – precise, objective description is all that is required at this stage. They should avoid metaphor, symbolism, interpretation, etc. but if anyone accidentally slips some in, no real need to worry. We are simply assembling a set of impressions in more or less concrete language – the description can be long and include as much detail as possible. In the second part of the exercise, students are asked to re-use any parts of the resulting descriptive language, phrases, and images, but this time they must write about a memorable event in their life, something that produced strong emotions in them. Teachers can decide if they will stipulate that the event be a troubling one; I will simply note that the exercise is more powerful if it is. The resulting writing pieces are often remarkably effective and affective due to the way concrete language is used to convey feeling.

Research suggests that, contrary to popular belief, this generation of students is particularly adept at pitching their writing through rhetorical devices so as to address a particular audience or reader. To engage and exercise this ability as well as to maintain student interest, instructors might therefore encourage them to direct their writing to an audience other than their professor or teacher. In order to take avail of this skill among the generation of so-called digital natives to discern changing contexts for their communication, teachers could fine-tune it as a way of coping better during times of crisis. Before assigning a paper to your students, consider initiating a discussion about what makes for an engaging and interesting conversation. The same principles apply to writing as they do to conversation but allow the students to suggest what those principles might be, perhaps by asking them to jot them down on post-it notes and leave them on the wall as they exit the classroom for a break or by posting them on a shared Google document if you are teaching online. You might even like to use these notes as the basis for writing goals by posting them on Poll Everywhere or a similar app for creating online polls and have everyone vote for their three favourite principles. These then become the principles they can apply in their writing assignments.

Also here, as with any reading of the quest novel in which the reader discovers the weird and wonderful, I recommend a post-seminar reflection activity by which students are asked to share their own encounters in which they have engaged in an act of learning with non-human life, be it in the process of learning how to keep "the Mother" alive for brewing kombucha or understanding the behavioural patterns of their pets by learning to interpret their body language. I suggest asking students to identify and analyse moments of these quest narratives and entanglements with non-human species as scenes of instruction.

Notes

1 Sascha Dannenberg and Theresa Grapentin, "Education for Sustainable Development – Learning for Transformation. The Example of Germany." Elsewhere, *Gestaltungskompetenz* refers to "the skills, competencies and knowledge to change economic, ecological and social behaviour" for the long duration with the view of making "an open future possible that can be actively shaped and in which various options exist" (de Haan 320).
2 http://writing.upenn.edu/library/Mayer-Bernadette_Experiments.html

2

CASE STUDY TWO

What the coming-of-age story teaches us about the Anthropocene

Texts: *The Catcher in the Rye; Brown Girl Dreaming; Song of Solomon; Never Let Me Go*

A teenager is adrift in New York. He has been expelled from boarding school and is unwilling to come home, besieged by feelings of self-doubt, frustration, and deep disappointment with friends and authority figures. The grief from his brother's death some four years earlier still weighs on him. Everything that he was taught as a child, that the world is generally a safe, loving, and comfortable place, he now thinks must be false. He feels as if he is disappearing in a superficial society in which most adults and youth alike are "phonies." Wondering where the ducks in the lake in Central Park go in winter, he might as well be wondering where there is shelter for the likes of him as he sheds the final pretence of innocence and awakens to the realities of adulthood.

I invoke the loneliness and existential despair felt by Holden Caulfield in Salinger's *The Catcher in the Rye* (2019[1951]), inseparable from his profound disappointment and mistrust of almost all of his fellow human beings, in order to draw parallels with the contemporary human predicament today. We are entering an epoch of climate change such that we can no longer feel safe in the knowledge that the world will continue to provide shelter for us and our children. We endure frustration and rage at the spectacle of leaders who pretend either that there is no crisis or that business can continue despite it. In important ways, a painful coming-of-age story such as Holden's parallels our present transition. Post-industrial society has largely been shaped by the affordances and comforts of a high energy expenditure and those of us who have benefited from it have lived a sheltered life under the protection of what fossil fuel can provide. Now that we are beginning to wake up to the realisation that we can no longer afford a lifestyle that is depleting the world's resources, we must grow up fast to move beyond this towards a more sustainable way of life. In this case study, I suggest applying critical literacy reading practices to the coming-of-age story so as to be able to teach the Anthropocene as a species-wide coming-of-age story. This grows out of the observation that many recent stories aimed at young adults are set against a backdrop of climate change or comparable widespread societal transition in which "coming of age" involves individual youth as well as culture as a whole.

In my first case study I explored the notion of "enduring understandings" (Wiggins and McTighe) – and specifically the insight that crisis can be a time of personal expansion and growth – as the basis for discovering the weird and the wonderful through reading literature that features the quest motif. Now, I show how the searching perspectives of youth that crystallise in the coming-of-age story can be used to teach critical literacy as a basis for the personal and cultural change that is necessary for responding to crisis. Hilary Janks stipulates that her critical literacy framework begins with the awareness that while language can be used to "persuade" and "deceive," this is inseparable from the ability to "construct … and produce representations of the world" (qtd in Turner and Griffin 319). Janks' approach to teaching literacy aims to empower students with the insight that a *diverse* range of social positions exist and they offer unequal levels of agency or *power*. With this comes the awareness that *access* to opportunities or "life chances" is dependent on social position. These components of her model – "*power, diversity, access*" (320) – contribute to the fourth component of her model which is "*design/redesign*," by which whatever is critiqued or deconstructed at the level of social reality can, via the means of language, be redesigned. As she says, "once you've deconstructed a practice or a text or a behavior, or anything that's taken for granted, what do you do about it? And that's the redesign process that leads to social action" (321). Ultimately, for Janks critical literacy "is about language practices, literacy practices, and social practices we construct or design" (319).

Through the example of Toni Morrison's *Song of Solomon*, among others, I also show how the coming-of-age story presents emotional literacy as being of immense value to the community as a whole during difficult times. This is because students are complex beings "made up of interacting minds, bodies, spirits, emotions, and so on," as Paul Hanstedt argues in his book *Creating Wicked Students: Designing Courses for a Complex World* (1). Here, I find it useful to refer to what Sardar M. Anwaruddin calls critical affective literacy after Patricia Clough's notion of "the affective turn" in the humanities and social sciences. The coming-of-age story teaches students strategies necessary for dealing with risk and for undergoing individual transformation and socio-historical paradigm shifts. In addition to critical literacy skills, sophisticated competency skills of spoken, written, and design rhetoric are also required for citizens to respond to a world that is undergoing radical socio-cultural, political, and environmental change.

What emerges in coming-of-age novels such as Jacqueline Woodson's *Brown Girl Dreaming* (2016[2014]) is the importance of adaptive strategies, including courage and resilience, to help find enough purpose in crisis to cultivate the strength for transformation. As we shall see, the coming-of-age genre can teach us about the significance of growth spurts and transition not just for an individual but also for communities or our species as a whole. This case study introduces reading practices that see crisis and related socio-economic shifts as processes that are unfolding rather than a set of fixed conditions. Beyond that, examples of the genre increasingly offer lessons for a civilisation that is slow to respond and adapt to the threat of cataclysmic events. Importantly, teachers will also acquire methods for inspiring hope through reading. One way this is achieved is when they learn the extent to which the narrative treatment of time and scale reveals the Anthropocene itself as a coming-of-age story rather than a story of inevitable decline.

The form of close reading that will be offered in this case study recognises the transformative potential of critical reading skills that eschew analysing a literary text as artefact and instead engage with it in a deeply personal way. Following Louise Rosenblatt's idea that the "teacher of literature, especially, needs to keep alive this view of the literary work as personal evocation, the product of creative activity carried on by the reader under the guidance of the text" (1000), this case study underscores the significance of the reader's experience of his or her own world such as it is. In relation to Janks, the case study also includes an active orientation towards what further that world might become through the reader's own agency. My claim is that this shift in attention – that incorporates aspects of Janks' and Rosenblatt's methods – has the most profound impact on the ability of students to gain from their reading the confidence to use language to bring realistic change into the world.

Teachers need to find a balance between negotiating the crisis as an opportunity for change and at the same time responsibly owning the serious nature of events, be it the pandemic, the climate, or threat to democracy. What is required is a pedagogy in transition, one that does not succumb to the doom and gloom stories, but rather sees the classroom for what it is: the making of a future otherwise than what presently is. While the coming-of-age story is about the maturation of an individual, the most memorable of such stories are those that create links between the self and others in the sense that the protagonist learns to live in connection with, dependency on, and responsibility to others. Crisis raises serious ethical questions for critical literacy to tackle. Consider for example the rhetoric of sustainability. What cultural traditions, means of livelihood, patterns of trade, political formations (and so on) should be sustained? This leads inevitably to the question of *who* should be sustainable. Which ethnic groups, populations of workers, strata of society, professional bodies, educational institutions, service providers, age groups (and so on) are considered essential and thus worth preserving even if at the expense of others? This is a question brought into sharp focus in Kazuo Ishiguro's *Never Let Me Go* (2005), as it depicts a world in which human clones are produced for the purpose of having their organs harvested to prolong the lives of their progenitors.

The Catcher in the Rye

The Catcher in the Rye is a novel steeped in trauma, emerging in the wake of the Second World War with a young man fighting for his adolescent life on the battlefield of the streets of New York and against the ignorance and conformity of the middle classes in whose charge he finds himself. Salinger wrote the opening chapters of the novel as he was serving in the army in the fight against Nazi Germany (Benson 1). A sense of extreme vulnerability and exposure permeates the pages of his iconic novel making it an ideal dream catcher for the visible and invisible strains and tensions our teaching and learning community now suffers. I think of the text together with these tensions – part of the contemporary social setting as well as the young reader's highly relevant stage of development – as a composite *said*. Recall in the Introduction I referred to Levinas for whom a creative or productive way of responding to what is, which he refers to as the *said*, is to seek what is otherwise than that in the form of a new form of *saying* (1). My initial aim then is to invite students to respond in their own words and to help them formulate this with increasing clarity in the direction of a *saying* in the form of an expression of their responsibility to each other now and to the future that must be otherwise than now. A course which includes the *Bildungsroman* benefits enormously from scaffolding the knowledge that students bring into the classroom. I usually begin a discussion on the coming-of-age story with a *visualisation* exercise addressed to the passage of time. Students are asked to jot down some notes in response to the following questions that focus on a time 30 years in the future.

Imagine the year 2050. You might be around 50 years of age.
It is Monday morning and you are about to do whatever it is you do for a living. What could that be?
Where are you living? What does it look like? Who else lives there?
Do you leave home in the morning? How do you get to where you are going?
What do you do during the day? Who do you meet there? What do you have for lunch?
In the evening you relax. What do you do?

   Students in the past have always been more or less able and willing to imagine their future selves, filling in the unknown with the plausible built on the familiar. Recently, however, I discovered that the majority of the class was unable to move beyond the first question. Unfortunately, I am not alone in this discovery. In the recently published *A Field Guide to Climate Anxiety*, Sarah Jaquette Ray similarly observes how her students were unable to visualise a future when responding to being asked "what it would feel and look like to live in a climate-changed future in which all the positive results of all their collective efforts had come to pass" (2). I echo Ray's concern that we need to teach students how to engage with crisis and not turn away from it. Bereft of any guidance, Holden Caulfield is left to travel the long dark night of the soul on his own. He no longer finds solace in the public buildings that once comforted him. The Museum of Natural History, previously a safe haven – "it always smelled like it was raining outside, even if it wasn't, and you were in the only nice, dry, cozy place in the world" (130) – now fills Holden Caulfield with revulsion. "I wouldn't have gone inside for a million bucks. It just didn't appeal to me" (131). *Close reading* might focus on what kind of solace a museum offers, why this is harder to access during turbulent times, and what this suggests about how Caulfield responds to change. If students have found it difficult to imagine their future, bring this discussion of the novel to bear on that blockage. Does crisis throw doubt on familiar taxonomies or systems of classification? What is the basis of trust in the future?

After an initial focus on how a passage like this addresses the adolescent's fear of change during times of great upheaval, I suggest moving beyond these sombre reflections. *The Catcher in the Rye* also tells of Holden's underlying maturation process towards freedom from preconceptions and judgment. The learning outcome for reading this novel in times of crisis draws on its insights into Holden's perception that the world is a relentlessly hostile place, and the reader's discernment that this perception of adversity and hostility is founded on his emotionally based preconceptions about events and people. To this aim, teachers might recognise with Hilary Janks that critical literacy alone, as a rational activity, "does not sufficiently address the non-rational investments that readers bring with them to texts and tasks" (*Literacy* 211). Taking these investments into account can make visible the range of emotional responses mobilised in times of crisis. Ultimately, this will encourage students to create their own storied representations that give them distance and perspective on their own emotional experiences. This will develop students' capacity to see others with less unnecessary fear and mistrust and pave the way to imagining futures in which they will contribute together.

The practice of othering underpinned by judgmental projections is the basis for a range of social ills such as scapegoating, which is more common during times of crisis as people compete for resources and the survival of their own kin. Escalation can ensue when judgmental behaviour elicits further judgment. Thus, students often remark on Holden Caulfield's projections of his own frustration onto other people and, for quite rational reasons, female students reject how he sometimes in the process negatively judges their gender. These are valid readings but they can overlook such aspects as Caulfield's position of vulnerability and exposure to danger that promotes his attitudes and further alienation from society. To foster a more tolerant attitude to others (tolerance being a form of resilience) I follow suggestions from Teresa Brennan. As Brennan notes in *The Transmission of Affect* (2004), thinking oneself separate from others is a learned illusion and consequently it can be unlearned by "examining the affects experienced in judging another" (119). This is an introspective pathway out of oneself, to a more open acceptance of others that does not see them as necessarily alien or hostile. Rather than judging and thus being possessed by affect, Brennan suggests discernment, "to know where one stands, to be self-possessed" (119). For those of us who teach literary studies, we know that literature provides an excellent arena for such tools of discernment to be taught via critical literacy skills attuned to details of character, context, social and historical setting, and so on.

For Brennan, "Discernment, in the affective world, functions best when it is able to be alert to the moment of fear or anxiety or grief or other sense of loss that permits the negative affect to gain a hold" (119). Brennan notes that discernment "works by feeling (sometimes in the dark), and it works deductively, often with insufficient information" (120). Although it "registers as a feeling" that can be articulated with more or less exactitude, as such it "requires a vocabulary" (120). I use an exercise that aims to capture Holden Caulfield's own process of growing discernment in the novel via the vocabulary of feeling emerging in the narrative and detaching itself from affect.[1] The following *channelling words* activity yields surprising results.

Ask students to select half-page passages from across the novel starting with the first page. These passages will be sources of emotion-laden words. Divide the class into groups of three – use virtual or "break-out" groups if teaching online. Ask Student A to read a sentence, Student B to repeat aloud a word that conveys significant emotional meaning for them from the sentence just read. It is not necessary to be able to name the emotion. Student B then reads the next sentence from the selected passage and Student A repeats one word from that sentence that resonates with them. Meanwhile, Student C records the words generated from this exercise and later shares them with the rest of the class. When completed, the class should be able to see on a shared whiteboard the columns of channelled words as a set of data for analysis. They can then analyse the changes in the emotional content of the narrative voice by distinguishing feeling words from those that express affect.

Initially, this exercise focuses on the reader's sensibility to offer direct insight into the operation of language for expressing feeling and affect. Any insights gained will be directed back to an examination of the novel. Since Salinger's intentions are not the direct focus of the exercise (nor at this stage are Caulfield's feelings or affects), I'm reminded of Roland Barthes' famous declaration of the death of the author, although perhaps not quite the endorsement of a reader "without history, without biography, without psychology" (6). When doing the *channelling words* activity, students are encouraged to *listen* instinctively and intuitively to the text as read to them by another, rather than relying only on their own cognitive abilities when reading silently and in private. In this sense, the reading is then more of a shared activity to start with, and the words eventually channelled are a literally collaborative measure of how multiple readers have responded to the text. In our case, as we channel words, we are certainly sidelining the author as well as many other traditionally respected objects of literary study such as plot, theme, character, and narrative voice. In fact, the object of enquiry that shows up in this exercise and subsequent discussion is not anything about the text as such but, rather, it is the raw data for mapping the emotional reactions of the class overall.

Teachers do not need to elaborate Brennan's theory in its own terms during this exercise. It is enough for them to know that the word lists rapidly assembled by their students in this process will comprise selections sometimes based on "fear or anxiety or grief or other sense of loss" (i.e. affect) and sometimes chosen with more discernment. We know the narrator of this story is in pain – perhaps for a lost innocence, as many critics contend. We also know that students of a certain age group may suffer in similar ways. Nevertheless, we aim to direct their reading powers to find interpretations that are not bound to their pain. One way of completing the exercise is to work (at least) twice with the words. In the first pass, use them as though they each refer to a profoundly felt loss of some kind and draw whatever significances can be read in them. Then take a more creative or even playful approach, one that makes no assumption regarding the emotional baggage attached to each word. When analysed, the resulting columns of words have the potential to visually illustrate that the words of Holden Caulfield's that stand out to a listener are also the bulwark necessitated by his vulnerable existence that keeps him isolated when trying to engage with his crisis. By catching and pinning those words to the shared wall for our attention, it emerges that *The Catcher in the Rye* is about the yearning not so much to find shelter, but to give shelter, to be the catcher in the rye.

Brown Girl Dreaming

The kind of deep listening practised in order to pick up on the content and emotional resonance of Holden Caulfield's narrative can be developed by learning to listen more empathetically to voices from the past. Jacqueline Woodson's memoir in poetic form, *Brown Girl Dreaming*, is focused on the United States of the 1960s and 1970s, a time when the civil rights movement gained strength in fighting racial segregation and injustice such as had been until then legitimated in so-called Jim Crow laws. This historical context greatly impacted Woodson's childhood and family life in South Carolina. *Brown Girl Dreaming* helps students consider ways by which their own coming-of-age narratives are shaped by where they live and the times the live through. Although this narrative poem is mostly included in syllabi for children's literature or on reading lists for teacher trainees, I refer to it here as a reminder of the value of storytelling for communicating ideas and learning.

Storytelling appears all too seldom on literature courses, whether structured thematically, through genre or period. This is a shame, especially in times of crisis when we more than ever rely on the ability to construct narrative sense out of what often feels like broken shards of existence. Sandra P. M. Ribeiro et al. remind us of the pedagogical importance of storytelling in their work in higher education on emotion expressed through digital storytelling: "Stories evoke in all engaging participants unexpected emotions, ideas and ultimately, unexpected selves, shifting perspectives on experience, constructing and deconstructing knowledge" (156). To make room for storytelling in the literature classroom, teachers may choose to engage students' own coming-of-age stories through a *story circle*, in which participants take turns telling a story from their own lives while the others listen. This, Ribeiro et al. note, is the basis also for the *individual digital story*, which they suggest, drawing on Lambert, need only consist of a voice-over and self-sourced photographs about a specific moment or event in a person's life (159).

While a *story circle* might work in some situations, I recommend putting structural limits on the activity for both your and the students' comfort such as providing a formal prompt. The following *story prompt* activity is a combination of the often-used George Ellen Lyon poem "Where I'm From" and Woodson's opening words "I am born" from *Brown Girl Dreaming*. It is designed to let a formal constraint promote creativity when practising life-writing. I give my students additional prompts: WHERE were they born? And WHEN? What time of day, what day of the year, what year, in what historical period? WHO lives or lived where they were born? WHAT happens or has happened there? HOW do they relate to that place now? Students are asked to come up with five statements each beginning with "I am born."

Song of Solomon

Storytelling is also at the heart of Toni Morrison's works. *Song of Solomon*, particularly, reverberates with storied knowledge as the motif of flight and flying is passed on from generation to generation. The young man at the heart of this *Bildungsroman*, Milkman, is told that "only birds and airplanes could fly." As a result, "he lost all interest in himself" (9). To compensate for this lack of ability to soar in the sky, his life spirals out of control in an attempt to "fly" in an allegorical sense, be it to rise above his circumstances through wealth or to escape his societal duties and family responsibilities. For critic Karen Carmen, Milkman's ability to tell his own story is central to his growing up. It is only then he discovers "an entirely different way of relating to people and places" (101). For Carmen, Milkman's rite of passage is intimately tied with his ability to relate to nature. At first, she notes, Milkman assumes superiority over nature and fails "to pay attention to nature's language" (103). It is only when he loses his possessions in the woods outside Shalimar that Milkman understands that "His watch and his two hundred dollars would be of no help out here, where all a man had was what he was born with, or had learned to use. And endurance" (276–277). Thus, in Milkman's coming-of-age story, he questions a much larger culture-wide narrative we sometimes tell our youth in which upward mobility is a sign of maturation. His questioning coincides with his deepening understanding of the role of language rooted in "a time when humans and animals shared communication" as well as his desire for wholeness in "shared relationships between men and women" (Carmen 104, 105).

To find freedom from having to repeat the story of upward mobility, Milkman must acquire knowledge of other kinds of wings from Pilate. She has stripped her existence to the bare essentials and freed herself from culturally constructed assumptions about identity. No longer weighed down by the restraints of an anthropocentric worldview, Pilate is able to communicate with all living things in this world as well as with the spirits of the departed. The narrative arc of Milkman's encounter with Pilate translates into a scene of instruction for moving beyond the simple knowledge that human material existence has contributed to the Anthropocene. By *close reading* various moments in this narrative, we see a shift in perception of what constitutes wellbeing and abundance, on one hand, and crisis and scarcity, on the other. Such insights are hard to discern in times of crisis, but one way available is via storytelling since values are conveyed and kept alive through such cultural structures. From a pedagogical point of view, the *learning to fly* lesson is about gaining a broader perspective as though seen from a height. It is an antidote to the tunnel vision that acute moments of crisis tend to cause with an emphasis on proximate relations, immediate security and short-term objectives. The fear associated with crisis tends to make us gravitate towards the familiar with the desire to return to "normal" often seen in public discourse after the initial phases of the Covid-19 pandemic. For Milkman, a return to normal would mean a return to a patriarchal, militaristic worldview as espoused by his friend Guitar. There are two parts to the *learning to fly* activity, both involving a shared whiteboard and active learning that engages and develops critical affective literacy.

First ask the students to come up with character traits (you could call them flying skills) that they think are important for "rising above" difficulties. They will award the three main characters in the novel – Milkman, Guitar, and Pilate – a score out of ten that rates them for having these qualities. It is fine to allow an element of humour or fantasy in selecting character traits; I have even suggested that they think of the qualities a superhero might have such as physical strength, adaptability, courage, or leadership, but they could also add "skill in delivering one-liners." This is sure to be an engaging and sometimes a fun way to spring-board into a discussion about the role of character in times of crisis. Aim to gather about five sets of scores and so place students in groups that divide the class this way. Put each group's scores for the characters on a whiteboard or a digital board such as http://scrumblr.ca/. The following are somewhat random numbers to indicate how the result might appear when tabulated:

	Milkman	Pilate	Guitar
Physical strength	6,8,3,7,5	5,5,4,8,6	8,4,7,6,5
Adaptability	7,2,5,3,7	8,5,8,6,3	5,2,6,7,5
Courage	7,8,7,7,6	9,8,7,8,6	5,5,4,6,7
Leadership	4,5,4,3,6	9,6,5,7,8	4,2,4,5,4

In the whole-class discussion that follows, members of each team can cite aspects of the story they referred to in making their assessments. They can argue for their scores and take on new insights from different groups. There are no correct scores. People may not agree on the definition of a strength, and in any case the purpose of the exercise is to understand how the text provides readable evidence for strengths – however they are understood – that help characters to overcome difficulties.

I add a second tier to this exercise that I call learning to *really* fly, which examines character strengths more realistically in relation to external factors. Here, the purpose is to provide critical and emotional perspective on what constrains or liberates the character traits so as to produce an *identity* within a social context. We still work with character in the novel since this has a literary bearing on who students are or hope to become (or avoid becoming). And I am still interested in how identity is articulated in the novel as something capable of surprising growth spurts, but I add to this some "systems thinking" about the ways identity is inscribed and constrained by public discourse. This part is inspired by the call to interrogate binaries and deconstruct the forces that fix our identity as explained by Eve Kosofsky Sedgwick in her chapter "Queer and Now" in *Tendencies* (1994).

In class, I refer to Sedgwick's lists of family and sexual identity headings in which she shows how identity is often caught in a predetermined web of discursive bonds. Sedgwick explains how "discourses of power and legitimacy" use terms such as "religion, state, capital, ideology, domesticity" (6). We discuss Sedgwick's ideas with an eye on how they relate to such matters as social demands or responsibilities, roles that people play, peer group pressure, wider scale oppression. We deal with injustice but we do not ignore the benign aspects of social constraints or obligations that shape or curb the expression of character in the formation of a socially recognised identity. I ask student groups to come up with a list of constraints relevant to the characters we have been studying – they can use any of Sedgwick's if they want. Then I ask them to review the previous results and think about how an awareness of the social constraints or duties that impact a given character might allow for a different assessment of that character's strengths.

There are two broad learning outcomes for this exercise. One is that students can develop a more forgiving way of reading what might otherwise seem to be weaknesses or flaws in character. Related to this, the other outcome is that students gain a sense of how social pressure affects individuals and how they can push back against unjust pressures to conform or toe the line. Further to that, the exercise suggests ways to redesign these identity-fixing structures on the lookout for more networked, collaborative ways of relating to each other.

A final note on Morrison's novel is that it *taxonomises*, evaluating and listing affordances in order to assess the value of things and the status of those who possess them. In chapter 3 of *Song of Solomon*, Railroad Tommy offers a litany of things that Guitar and Milkman will never have. It includes, among other things, "a sweet woman, clean sheets, and a fifth of Wild Turkey." Tommy tells them that though, as black men, they might "shoot down a thousand German planes" single-handedly "and land in Hitler's backyard and whip him with your own hands [...] you never going to have four stars on your shirt front, or even three" (59–60). The items on the list provoke a sobering discussion about inequality and oppression as systematically ingrained in society and culture. Through *close reading*, students can be invited to analyse the items on Railroad Tommy's list. What do women and whisky signify, or stars on one's shirt? What specific aspects of society and culture are Guitar and Milkman barred from due to racial discrimination?

Never Let Me Go

Crisis often reveals systemic inequality including patterns of oppression and discrimination. In a highly nuanced treatment of these themes, Ishiguro's dystopic *Never Let Me Go* is a coming-of-age story depicting young adult humans who have been cloned in order to supply their genetic originals with transplant organs. In other words, the novel shows people objectifying others who can be understood as barely different from themselves – arguably they are identical others. The novel can be read allegorically about unequal privilege and the consequences of taking advantage of people within a class system. It poses ethical questions especially relevant for times of crisis by asking whether it is ever acceptable to preserve one group of people (e.g. a culture, a class, an age group, or ethnic group) at the expense of another. The novel is a warning to readers that the rhetoric used to discuss options during crisis must be interrogated as well as the ultimate goals that are assumed to be worthwhile. Should we aim for survival of our own group at all costs? Similarly, the word *sustainability* is sometimes taken for an unquestioned good, but perhaps it is not always for the best. The young people coming of age in the novel are affordances of a wealthy class who harvest organs from them when needed. This would suggest that the wealthy people's lives are thus more sustainable, though this clearly raises the question of whether or not the whole process should be sustained.

In class, I draw attention to the words of the novel's title, "never let me go." They are also the title of what, on the face of it, is a love song, a favourite of the central character, Kathy, who thinks the song is about a newborn baby. This is a poignant reminder for the reader of Kathy's motherless origin as a clone. A more conventional interpretation of the song would be that it is a plea to a lover and thus is part of the discourse of sexual or romantic love that – like birth, babies, or parenting – is also alien to a clone. I focus discussion on the word "me." In the context of potential human cloning in the world beyond the novel, the question of who "me" might refer to is immediately and no doubt intentionally ambiguous since, as we know, a clone is a non-sexually reproduced genetic *duplicate* of someone derived from their DNA. If I could beget a clone, is it (or he or she) really other than "me"?

This helps me to steer the discussion beyond the two interpretations of who – baby or lover – speaks the words "never let me go." It is a good opportunity to talk about the basics of literary representation at the junction of realism and allegory, poetics and rhetoric, fiction and non-fiction. At this time, I can also remind students that readers of literature are invited to challenge the notion that texts are stable entities or that they have single correct meanings. This all helps students to understand that the words "never let me go" for them as readers of the novel are meant to have much deeper and variable significance than would be available to the fictional Kathy or even for the song's fictional author, Judy Bridgewater.[2]

With students sufficiently primed by the foregoing discussions, I use answerga rden.ch or any other platform that shapes answers into word clouds to generate a quick, visual representation of how they respond (as many times as they like) to the question, "Who or what is being asked to 'never let me go'?" and "Who might that *me* refer to?" This is developed in *think, pair and share* group work, either on a collaborative tool such as Google Docs or face-to-face. I get students to discuss among themselves the corporeal basis of selfhood. Questions can be: Is there an irreducible "me" separate from my bodily configuration? What bodily parts can I lose without losing personhood? Am I still the same me if I receive an organ transplant? A question especially interesting for users of digital services is, to what extent does my use of social networking and online entertainment define who I am? As part of this, I aim to discuss the aspects of personality or character that express some independence from their biological basis and that will serve students well, especially in crisis – traits such as resilience, courage, generosity, creativity. This is not to deny the importance of relationships and community and indeed qualities that define an individual are also part of what that person can bring to any kind of concerted endeavour.

Character takes on an unusual significance in this novel that subtly affirms the thorough materiality of all that is human. Is the contemporary human materially formed by technological and cultural processes? On one hand, the events and written form of the narrative point to what we usually think of as character in the human terms that place it above or beyond the simple bodily configuration of persons. On the other hand, the fact that the story is told by a clone and is about the hopes and despairs of clones, reminds us that whatever we are construing as independent of materiality happens to beings who are the products of biotechnology coupled with economic business interests that provide services to those who can afford them. The novel thematises the tragic plight of an underclass struggling to live as fully as possible under severe limitations regarding the influence they can have on the conditions under which they live.

Ultimately, strong points of resonance can be identified between the clones in the story and ourselves as historically, economically, technologically, and socially *produced* readers. Although we are not clones, we too have limited power to bring about significant change in the world due to the complexity and the momentum of the ongoing processes that produce and maintain that world and us in it. A question I try to encourage students to tackle considers that although the qualities and attributes possessed by "me" necessarily vary from person to person, the rights and obligations of the person concerned need not differ because of these biological (or class-based, ethnic, racial, etc.) differences.

Students are aware that the world and its problems are usually described using concepts such as cause and effect, intention, conflict, and resolution. These are terms that literary scholars engage with every day using narrative analysis. Key to making literary studies keenly relevant for students is the understanding that they can learn how the world works through their reading. Moreover, reading practices that demonstrate how interpretations and choices drive the dynamics of prolonged historical sequences as well as rapidly unfolding social processes are useful in times of crisis. At the same time, there is no rule of representation or clarification that gives readers access to simple answers. This is about teaching students to become comfortable with complexity or even confusion knowing only that it is fundamentally readable and open to interpretation as well as intervention. Students also need to be taught a critical affective literacy that ultimately lets them respond to feelings that grow out of the events they witness without succumbing to the strong pull of less mediated affects such as rage, grief, or despair. This frees them to explore ethical issues in specific and concrete terms. In light of this, I favour writing exercises that encourage students to write back to what they have read. Here is where they can create novel and plausible alternative outcomes for the stories they read. This provides them with a skill not just for reading but for living creatively even during crisis.

As preparation for a writing exercise, I draw attention to the emotionally flat narrative style of Kathy's account for clues about the different forms of expression that her cloned subjectivity takes. I suggest that students may trace the way she perceives her physical world throughout her memoir. Kathy gives testimony of the deaths of her loved ones as well as the existential questions faced by them in life. She also strives to reconstruct the events of the past, perhaps even seeking to make room for the power of the imagination to create a different future. It is important that students be reminded of the role of the imagination in challenging the notion that endings are predetermined. I turn to the touching and rather sombre conclusion of Ishiguro's novel in which Kathy engages in a moment of restrained fantasy. I invite students to do a *close reading* of this passage:

> I was thinking about the rubbish, the flapping plastic in the branches, the shore-line of odd stuff caught along the fencing, and I half-closed my eyes and imagined this was the spot where everything I'd ever lost since my childhood had washed up, and I was now standing there in front of it, and if I waited long enough, a tiny figure would appear on the horizon across the field, and gradually get larger until I'd see it was Tommy, and he'd wave and maybe even call. The fantasy never got beyond that – I didn't let it – and though the tears rolled down my face, I wasn't sobbing or out of control. I just waited a bit, then turned back to the car, to drive off to wherever it was I was supposed to be.
>
> *(282)*

I help students to notice that emotions are suppressed, possibly not because Kathy cannot acknowledge the poignancy of this moment of glimpsing a fantasy and letting it go, but because she chooses to let it go. Politically, her position could be called quietist – she will not fight for clones' rights. I suggest that this is a legitimate mode of survival under conditions that cannot be altered. I also draw attention to the opening imagery of rubbish and ask of its significance. Are there other, deeper feelings concealed beneath Kathy's resignation? The writing exercise is called *what if?* In smaller discussion groups, I invite students to come up with just a few alternative character traits for Kathy – even one can be sufficient – that would be the basis of different feelings or reactions in her or a different mode of expressing them. I ask them to think about how the difference they are imagining for her might influence the options available to her. These considerations can feed into an essay-length assignment. Students could rewrite the passage cited or another one of their choice and make slight changes to it so as to point out how character is indicated and how this enables the narrative plausibly to take alternate pathways. Arguably, Ishiguro's acclaimed and yet markedly pessimistic novel is a provocation to readers to think beyond the impasse its central characters face. I see it that way and set an essay question prompting discussion of the significance of the choices embedded in the novel's present form and the literary means and purpose of thinking otherwise than that.

Notes

1 In *The Feeling of What Happens* (1999), ch. 1, Antonio Damasio makes a comparable distinction between feeling as coherent and communicable and emotion as a diffuse bodily and neurological condition.
2 Kathy is a very interesting variation on an *unreliable narrator*. Her maturity and wisdom are the basis for her responsibilities for counselling her peers when they are ailing or in the expected terminal decline. Despite this, her education and upbringing prevent her gaining much knowledge or ethical insight into the predicament of clones as objects in the service of the rich. Can we think of real-world examples of people who are kept in the dark regarding political, economic, environmental (etc.) aspects of their existence?

3

CASE STUDY THREE

Things to do with the canon in the classroom

Texts: *The Adventures of Huckleberry Finn; Moby Dick;* **solarpunk fiction;** *Oliver Twist; Ship Breaker*

The author of *The Ocean in the School: Pacific Islander Students Transforming Their University*, Rick Bonus, recounts how his students were able to change "their idea, imagination, and practice of their school, because … they wanted to allow themselves and their communities to be constitutively woven into the very school that they sought to transform" (201). Bonus recalls with regret how the Pacific Islander students were accepted at their mainland university insofar as they added "diversity," but that they were in fact exploited or ridiculed "especially when they were seen to privilege collective practice over liberal individualistic behavior" (25). Teaching now must strive to do more than disseminate and reproduce knowledge, term after term, year after year. I begin this chapter on canonicity with this glimpse of Bonus' account of the hopes and challenges for transformative education in order to stress the importance in times of crisis of creating a classroom that takes its direction from students' aspirations to create community. My approach to the canon presents teachers with an opportunity to invite students to find communities of fellow readers with whom they can transform knowledge by resisting, repurposing, or otherwise renewing works often thought to exclude them due to the aura of high-cultural elitism frequently linked with canonicity.

In this chapter I focus on the teaching of canonical works of fiction via a less teacher-centred classroom model. This is because this case study assumes a blended or online delivery in which research has shown the teacher's gaze is less able to assess attentiveness. As noted by Derek Mueller, where "the lines blur between the traditional classroom, the computer-enabled classroom, and the worlds (real and virtual) at large," the once reliable "strict correspondence between attention and the gaze has come unhitched" (246). This is because the "economies of attention" of students are "attuned in a complex orchestration across highly varied attractions and playing at once across conceptual, material, and digital orders" (246). Mueller updates Robert Brooke's term "underlife" to refer to digitally enhanced "backchannels" in the classroom that manifest as "transgressions of institutional rules and roles manifest in writing – in the digital packets of discourse that are no longer confined by the physical space of a singular institutional scene" (241). Mueller traces Brooke's thinking here to the work of sociologist Erving Goffman, whose original concept of underlife signifies an area of subversive and creative self-invention that resists institutional labelling. For Goffman, this involves "the activities (or information games) individuals engage in to show that their identities are different from or more complex than the identities assigned them by organizational roles" (qtd in Mueller 243).

In light of this competition for students' attention, rather than attempting to counter the digital underlife, as said, I recommend that the canon can be taught by turning down the teacher-centred approach and instead making full use of any creative support to be found online. In what follows, I plan to re-route the readings of canonical works via such digital underlife and backchannel activities generated by readers of the canon in writing activities inspired by fan fiction as well as the coupling of the canon with lesser-known genre fiction. The aim is not to refer to the canon in order to defend the attention it receives in curricula around the world. Rather, I want to explore further what qualities are found in the canon that make it durable. Here, I want to use the term *perennial* although it is sometimes viewed askance in literary criticism. This may in part be because it seems to attribute an exalted or timeless quality to a text as though to uncritically accord the work an unquestioned permanent place in our literary hall of fame. This would be to place it beyond the reach of history by which at times it may be seen in an altogether different and less reverential light. That is not my intention though I do still insist on referring to the perennial quality of the canonical text. I use the problematic term with care: I stress that whatever makes a text so resilient as to be worthy of widespread respect and deep appreciation over decades or centuries is not its resistance to change but because it changes with the times, offering each generation of readers timely and fresh insights into their own times. I will return to this aspect of canonicity below since I believe that such expressions of literary resilience can show readers how to navigate the vicissitudes of crisis.

The Adventures of Huckleberry Finn

Fanfiction refers to stories penned by admirers of a particular author or text and set in that author's fictional world. Such writing is often presented in online forums of avid readers and contributors whose emotional and intellectual investment in both the original work and each other's spin-offs has the power to shape their own stories. Fanfiction is often rooted in the canon although, importantly, its relationship to the original work tends to be less compliant than, for example, an adaptation. This is not to say, however, that this writing is heedless of the original work. For reasons that have to do with the seemingly unchallenged superiority of the original, readers of fanfiction are sometimes treated as if they are less sophisticated readers preferring this genre to the original work. However, in thinking about how to teach literature in times of crisis, I suggest we need to look much more seriously at fanfiction for its capacity to support prolific and widespread communities of dedicated close readers and interpreters. These are, in my view, now playing a significant part in the resilience and endurance of the canon even if from a distal point in relation to academic scholarship.

I find that the fanfiction community structured around the principle of creative and respectful feedback loops serves as an excellent model for anyone wishing to create a learning space that promotes a high degree of interaction and encourages participation from the students. It turns out I'm not alone. Teacher and author of *Why Fanfiction Is Taking Over the World*, Anne Jamison, notes that:

> Fans, it often seemed, were paying more attention and saying smarter things than my Ivy League students .... They enjoyed attending closely and making arguments based on their observations. For all I knew, some of these fans *were* my students, but how could I get students to do this stuff *as* students?
>
> (7)

Let's find out, first of all, what it is that fans do as opposed to student readers. It might be useful to remember that fanfiction originates from the science fiction fandom of the 1960s – a community of mostly female science fiction enthusiasts who celebrated the practice of writing stories that borrowed material from already published stories (Coppa 2). Unlike other writers who write in order to eventually have their work published, these fans had no such ambition other than to share their attempts with each other. Instead, they used pre-existing stories as springboards for expanding the plot or otherwise tweaking it to encompass details that were thought to be missing in the original.

This practice of adding details that are missing or downplayed in the original stories, often to do with sexual practices, has evolved into a significant aspect of the popularity of this genre. LGBTQ fans are empowered to give voice to perceived undercurrents of non-normative sexual attraction between characters whom their original authors presented as straight. An excellent example I will develop is that of the friendship between Huckleberry Finn and Tom Sawyer in Mark Twain's novel *The Adventures of Huckleberry Finn*. While their comradeship is conventionally read through a heteronormative perspective, their friendship has generated highly nuanced fanfiction in which their feelings for each other are more than friendship. With this in mind, I have returned to Twain's novel, this time bringing to it the awareness that a young student reader might have who has not yet come out as a gay man.

On reading *Huckleberry Finn* this reader might be struck by the fullness of feeling expressed by Huck Finn as he worries about what his friend Tom stands to lose as a result of offering to help Huck rescue Jim, the run-away slave:

> Here was a boy that was respectable and well brung up; and had a character to lose; and folks at home that had characters; and he was bright and not leather-headed; and knowing and not ignorant; and not mean, but kind; and yet here he was, without any more pride, or rightness, or feeling, than to stoop to this business, and make himself a shame, and his family a shame, before everybody. I *couldn't* understand it no way at all. It was outrageous, and I knowed I ought to just up and tell him so; and so be his true friend, and let him quit the thing right where he was and save himself.
>
> *(465)*

Like many readers, he might identify with Huck Finn's awe at the true courage he sees in Tom Sawyer for doing what he believes is right. Huck's feeling is mixed with deep concern that Tom's actions could mean bringing shame to his family. This reader knows of other acts of courage, many of them true stories, and he also thinks about what it takes to come out in a community that does not accept homosexuality. He suddenly finds it plausible that Huck Finn and Tom Sawyer are romantically interested in each other, only their author wasn't game to suggest this himself on the page. The following is how this reader might follow up his interpretation.

> *I attempt a fanfiction to elaborate on this finding, choosing as a starting point the chapter in which the two boys spend the night at Aunt Sally's. It becomes a story of seduction that is still rather old-fashioned, the way any romance might have been at the time Twain wrote his novels. In other words, past reading informs my attempt. Just to be sure, I add a warning that the story contains homoeroticism so that visitors to my selected fanfiction site* [1] *have the choice not to read if they would be offended.*
>
> *As it turns out, I don't get enough comments on what I write so I soon abandon the project. Still, I had a lot of fun and it was a boost to my confidence to discover this new world of fellow readers and contributors. And once I got the idea from our alternative ways of reading, there was no stopping me. It opened up my eyes in the sense that I felt I was becoming a bit of a detective when I was reading, on the look-out for subtexts or outright cover-ups itching for fuller expression. Soon, in Twain's novel, I was following the gay theme from start to finish, including passages that included bed sharing and Tom even putting on Aunt Sally's dress that he stole (ch. 40). Later when I have to write an essay for this class, the teacher says I am a careful reader and that I have an eye for detail. I'm also told I have the ability to substantiate my argument using textual evidence from the book.*

Fanfiction communities are a strong support for individuals developing agency through their literary voice. This is especially true when crisis brings with it an extreme exposure to the fragility and vulnerability of the individual self. In an essay entitled "Sharing Vulnerabilities: Searching for 'Unruly Edges' in Times of the Neoliberal Academy," Monika Rogowska-Stangret identifies clear elements of crisis in the impact of the "neoliberal tempo" that obliges university students to attune their minds and bodies to its hectic and headlong pace (15) in the service of individualism and "virtues such as productivity, efficiency, and competition" (12). She notes that "Sleeplessness, constant activity, the impossibility to be passive, inert, or idle" are features of this condition. Following new materialists and feminists such as Karen Barad, Elizabeth Grosz, and Brian Massumi, Rogowska-Stangret sees a solution in their account of new distributions of subjective agency away from the traditional hierarchical locus of the embodied individual (16). The result is a radical yet viable form of agency "as a multitude, as a swarm of re/actions that reconfigure the world on macro and micro scales" (17). This agency can function as caring solidarity and a remade self "as always already collective" and fundamentally connected to "the zone of shared concerns and shared vulnerabilities" (21–22).

While Rogowska-Stangret is here speaking of teachers, this is also something that can be fostered in our students and modelled through the way we teach. And I see a version of prolific and distributed authorial agency that Roland Barthes would have approved in the fandom sites that engage so inventively and democratically with the literary canon. When teaching in times of crisis, it is important to be even more attentive than usual to the passions and powers students already bring into the classroom and scaffold those skills and interests. This doesn't necessarily mean making space in a course for writing fanfiction as such, but there are other exercises that create opportunities for students to bring their way of reading and writing into the classroom. By so doing, we as teachers open the doors for what the students do in their free time and create bridges between reading as fans and as students. These activities include confidence-building exercises, reading for pleasure, and shifting the responsibility for learning from teacher to student. To begin with, students need to be allowed to follow their interests when they are reading. This is at the heart of the popularity of fanfiction. For fans, reading is not a break from their interests and occupations, rather it becomes an endorsement of who they are. To dip into sites such as fanfiction.net and archiveofourown.org is to be among friends in a community of acceptance and support. It is worth remembering that fans are also able to practise critical literacy, but that it is more likely to occur on sites such as https://tvtropes.org/.

In times of crisis we need to make room for community and creativity in our classrooms. These are fostered through reading and writing practices. It makes a difference at the level of engagement if students are permitted to build a relationship with the canon in the same way that they engage with other texts in their lives outside the classroom. When teaching a canonical work of fiction such as *The Adventures of Huckleberry Finn* (or any other one for that matter), encourage your students to engage with it on their terms through a *recasting a scene* exercise. Draw their attention to a relevant passage from the novel and ask your students to adapt it for the movies. Prompt them with questions such as:

- Who would you cast in the main roles?
- Where would you set it?
- What visual features would you use to bring out your interpretation?
- Which symbolic object would you include to suggest a key theme in the scene?

This exercise could be adapted in the direction of fanfiction by simply suggesting that students outline in similarly broad terms how they would approach creating an elaboration and reworking of the scene that emphasises a narrative turn of their own. In any form, in this exercise students nevertheless get to think as fans – both readers and contributors. They also practise some of the formal reflections that come with their decisions and these can become the basis for a class discussion about such questions to do with interpretation and representation.

Essential to the techniques of fanfiction is the capacity to see literature, literary form, as a material that can be used inventively to make *new textual objects*. It is a skill and a playful way of looking at textuality that can be learned. An exercise that is usually extremely popular with students invites them to use language as raw material, which they are then free to adapt and repurpose for other uses. For instance, you can select a paragraph from a chapter or a story that you are studying and give this to your students with the instructions to write something different with the words available to them through this paragraph. I often ask them to write a love letter *or* a breakup letter with the language available. It is important to give them the possibility of doing either since they then get to demonstrate for themselves that the same subset of language can be put to opposite uses. It is not surprising that students often realise that this is an exercise in manipulating someone else's words, which then leads to a most productive conversation about more recent phenomena captured by such terms as "fake news" and "post truth."

Another method of developing competence in this area of seeing language creatively is to bring stories from a selection of newspapers to class for a *newspaper cut-ups* activity. An added advantage to this is that there is a chance to handle material things, which can be sorely missed in a digital classroom. Students can be responsible for bringing their own newspaper stories to the seminar if they are physically distanced from each other. Ask them to cut up their chosen story from the newspaper and rejoin phrases so that new meaning emerges. (It can be done entirely with paper and scissors with results shared to camera, or it may involve scanning text to share digitally.) This can be seen as a form of literary self-defence against the force of slogans, ideological content, bias, and catch phrases. It is a good classroom exercise for gaining an understanding of all kinds of verbal spin-doctoring from advertising to propaganda.

Fanfiction's focus on engagement with characters shows a way to build enduring relationships with works that have stood the test of time and it helps overcome resistance to what for many students are new and unfamiliar texts. This is important to remember in times of crisis as alienation and anxiety tend to make focusing on new work a challenge. When the students find it difficult to relate to a canonical work of literature that is often written in a more formal style, they may relax into the character world by putting together a *literary playlist* of songs to indicate a character's growth through the span of a few chapters or a whole novel. In the process of speaking to their playlist and comparing it with those of their peers, the students will find their way into a language of both creative playfulness and critical engagement with the text. In my experience, these literary playlists have provided readers with an emotional anchor to characters that have been otherwise difficult to understand. To conclude, exercises such as these are about helping students discover and build a set of narrative resources that encourage in them the readiness to step from what is familiar to them or to use existing competencies and take on the unfamiliar. In essence, they learn to develop and trust in their ability to engage with a troubled world.

Moby Dick

In this part of the case study, I design reading activities by putting select passages from Melville's *Moby Dick* in conversation with recent solarpunk fiction. This is a sub-genre that runs counter to the pessimism of the popular apocalyptic and cli-fi (climate fiction) genre with more hopeful representations of energy renewal often based, as the genre's names suggests, on actual or potential uses for solar energy. My reason for this pairing is twofold. I said above that part of what makes a work canonical is the kind of resilience that sees its themes remaining relevant to each generation's historical setting. Although attitudes to energy production have changed markedly since Melville wrote *Moby Dick*, his novel, centred as it is on an obsessive relationship with a source of fuel for lighting the newly industrialised world, speaks resonantly to our own concerns regarding energy. And so it interests me to see what emerges from drawing a correspondence between this central theme in the novel and the new genre of solarpunk, which is also concerned with the human need for sustainable light. I also said that many young readers view canonical literature with trepidation because of the assumed difficulty that attaches to its high-cultural status. No such difficulty applies to solarpunk fiction and so pairing it with Melville's novel is helpful as a means to gently introduce them to the marvels of Melville's prose.

When teaching literature in times of environmental crisis, it is especially rewarding to compare energy narratives from the beginning of the oil century with the speculative fiction of recent times. This is because students learn methods for assessing the shifting relationship between humans and energy, especially oil, and how this registers in our cultural imaginary. I rely on prompts such as the following representation of energy questions to bring such seminar discussions into focus:

- How do fictional characters register fear of energy, such as pollution, securitisation, contamination, etc?
- Is there a difference between how male and female characters represent different kinds of energy expenditure?
- How does the novel invite reflection on intimacy and energy?
- In what ways is the cost of energy figured in the decisions that characters make?

- How are energy sources described in terms of their impact on families, communities, minorities?
- How are "us" and "them" configured in relation to access to affordances?
- Does the writing aestheticize aspects of energy production? If so, how?
- What ethical choices do the characters make about energy?

When I teach *Moby Dick*, I draw attention to, among other things, the way Melville offers his readers a glimpse of what is meant by the civilising effect of the riches available from whale oil as a high-quality source of energy. I inform students of how the cities of Europe and America were lit up by sperm oil at the time Melville was writing his novel and how, no doubt, parts of his novel were written and read by the light of a spermaceti lamp. I do this to encourage students to consider sources of energy not just in terms of greenhouse gas emissions but also with a view to their affordances. By pairing chapter 97, "The Lamp," with solarpunk speculations on what sources of energy might look like in the future, I bring to awareness literature's role in imagining the culture that will pave the way for a transition to renewable energy sources. Narrative, myth, and stories are the social fabric of our existence. They found our engagement with the world and with each other. We can thus enlist the resources of the literary imagination to see beyond the habits of thought organised around the extraction, refinement, and consumption of oil and other fossil fuels, looking towards a post-carbon future. However, it is important when preparing for a future energy transition that the stories of energy are embedded within a community of practice that is diverse and inclusive. This is another reason why I put the canonical *Moby Dick* in conversation with solarpunk. Ultimately, the development of an entirely renewable energy system will require alternatives that may seem fictional today, but can turn out to be tomorrow's reality.

In "The Lamp," Melville compares the Pequod to "some illuminated shrine of canonised kings and counsellors" (401). Arguably, when Melville refers to light he has in mind its significance for appreciation of cultural traditions and possibly spiritual ones as well. Here, if not the light of wisdom necessary for the traditional pursuit of scholarly knowledge, I see at least the democratic light by which anyone may read the pious or literary classics, or even learn to read them, including the whaleman who "makes his berth an Aladdin's lamp." In other words, Melville is offering readers an idealised and indeed a rather enlightened view of energy consumption very different from the headlong pursuit of progress and the proliferation of commodities that have become a cause of anxiety in our late capitalist age. It is fair to say that Melville's narratives of oil evoke the idyll of productivity, wealth, ease, either as actual possibilities or as lost or threatened ideals. Aboard a whaler, Melville tells us, the sailor burns "the purest of oil, in its unmanufactured, and, therefore, unvitiated state; a fluid unknown to solar, lunar, or astral contrivances ashore. It is sweet as early grass butter in April." While sustainability in the sense we understand it today was unlikely to be on Melville's mind, there is an emphasis on pleasure constrained by measure in the interest of permanence and endurance. Earlier, in chapter 45, "The Affidavit," Ishmael details the perilous conditions for whalemen and finally addresses the reader directly, telling of his own experience of the sailors whose lives were lost on whaling ventures: "For God's sake," he implores, "be economical with your lamps and candles! not a gallon you burn, but at least one drop of man's blood was spilled for it" (198).

We can now fast forward into the brave new world of renewable energy as depicted in Jennifer Lee Rossman's solarpunk story, "Riot of the Wind and Sun" (2018). The story is set in the non-fictional central Australian opal-mining town of Coober Pedy over 800 kilometres from the capital. This town in the desert provides the larger urban centres with solar energy even as it is itself largely buried in darkness with a population that lives partially underground to survive the harsh daytime temperatures of the outback. In the near future of this story, the chief reason for Coober Pedy's existence is to provide solar energy to the capital leaving the outback unsupplied, "a black swath in the middle" of the continent (34). When the music band "Riot of the Wind and Sun" is rumoured to be circling the Australian continent by light plane scouting venues for a pop-up concert, a teenage girl, Kirra, decides she wants that event in her town. But first she needs to put Coober Pedy visibly on the map. She ends up gathering the people of the town in their glow clothes, the luminescent attire they wear to orient themselves in the dark "so they'd never be inconvenienced on days when the capital took all the power" (32). Then, she instructs them to lie down forming the name "Coober Pedy" on the ground with an arrow pointing to the town. In the end, she succeeds in redrawing the map, turning a sacrifice zone into the "hidden gem" of Australia (39).

The concluding image of the town emerging triumphantly from the darkness as "that little patch of light along the Stuart Highway" (39) corresponds well with a pair of images from *Moby Dick*. Melville contrasts the abundance of light on the Pequod with conditions on a merchantman where the sailor must "dress in the dark, and eat in the dark, and stumble in darkness to his pallet" whereas on the Pequod "the whaleman, as he seeks the food of light, so he lives in light … so that in the pitchiest night the ship's black hull still houses an illumination" (401). The point here is that by doing comparative readings between the canonical *Moby Dick* and solarpunk, teachers are able to bring resource extraction politics into view via literature of very different kinds.

Returning for a moment to the question of what makes a text canonical, what emerges is that while solarpunk emphasises the virtues of ingenuity and communal problem-solving, it is *Moby Dick* that justifies its place in the canon because of the epic scope of its narrative as well as its literary resourcefulness even despite the impact that the cruel violence of its depiction of whaling would have on contemporary readers. That said, by contemplating the representation of energy questions students will discover that the social order that is depicted in solarpunk fiction is by no means automatically more equitable and just simply because fossil fuels have been replaced with renewables.

Similarly, students will need to be shown that even digital activities are costly in terms of carbon-dioxide emissions, even though they are often thought of as "clean." There is no such thing as immaterial media, as media theorist Sean Cubitt reminds us

(13). Moreover, as shown by "Riot of the Wind and Sun," despite renewables, environmental justice problems follow a colonial pattern of exploitation whereby the outback in this case is transformed into a sacrifice zone there to service the urban centres with energy. One way of exposing the myth of immaterial media and bring resource extraction politics into view is to ask students to work out or even estimate the cost in carbon-dioxide emissions of their own digital activities. There are several online tools available that help in calculating how much CO2 one's lifestyle emits including Global Footprint Network and Kilo What? Ultimately, I hope for students to achieve more awareness of the uneven distribution of energy and its affordances and to attain a greater sense of responsibility for their digital consumerism through reflecting on its environmental impact.

An activity to do with your students involves *finding possible read-alikes* on the theme of the original text of study. These are books or stories that have themes similar to the ones that have emerged from the seminar discussions so far. Ask your students to compile a list of other books, but also cultural artefacts, articles, film titles, songs, comics, poems, anything that explores similar questions to do with energy, social justice, problem-solving, and affordances, to name a few themes that have been raised. As Williams reminds us, "literacy is not a stand-alone set of skills but social practices influenced by context and culture" (683). Our job then is to make our students more aware and able to identify these cultural practices. We can achieve this by bringing them into focus in the literature classroom.

As we shall see with Dickens in the next section, so with Melville, a significant feature of *Moby Dick* is the voice of its narrator, Ishmael, who is a character in his own right. This voice, though obviously informed by the wide ranging interests, years of experience and reading, and keen eye for human manners of its author, is still a character in a novel. What if this character were to be replaced by another narrator character from a different novel? Obviously, this *narrator crossing over* exercise can be done with any two texts and they don't both have to be canonical. Nevertheless, I do wonder how parts of *Moby Dick* would come across if told by Holden Caulfield, Nick Carraway, or Marlow of *Heart of Darkness*. For convenience here since we have been discussing Mark Twain, and with all respect due, I would suggest momentarily supplanting the inimitable narratorial style of Ishmael with the unique tones of Huckleberry Finn. Just to be clear though, there is no limit to the possible combinations you could choose from. Note that this crossing over exercise can be done with any characters, not just the one narrating. Whichever way it is done, it is an exercise most suited to students with already a keen interest in literature and hence significant wider reading than the texts you are teaching them. Obviously, this means they will have ideas of their own regarding which narrator they would like to imagine telling an unfamiliar tale.

For our purpose, there are many passages and whole chapters of *Moby Dick* that contain only Ishmael's voice as in the many devoted to the history and practice of whaling and those, often simply entitled "Cetology," that deal with practical knowledge of whales or their history. One of my favourite passages and one that might be suited to the sensitivity of Huck Finn is in chapter 87, "The Grand Armada." Here, Ishmael recounts how the

Pequod encountered an immense herd of thousands of whales that seemed to have formed a vast defensive circle within which were the young and mothers. From the whaling craft, surrounded by whales, Ishmael witnesses juvenile sperm whales approaching innocently: "Like household dogs they came snuffling round us, right up to our gunwales, and touching them; till it almost seemed that some spell had suddenly domesticated them" (365). Next, he recounts a wondrous sight of whale family life:

> far beneath this wondrous world upon the surface, another and still stranger world met our eyes as we gazed over the side. For, suspended in those watery vaults, floated the forms of the nursing mothers of the whales, and those that by their enormous girth seemed shortly to become mothers. The lake, as I have hinted, was to a considerable depth exceedingly transparent; and as human infants while suckling will calmly and fixedly gaze away from the breast, as if leading two different lives at the time; and while yet drawing mortal nourishment, be still spiritually feasting upon some unearthly reminiscence; – even so did the young of these whales seem looking up towards us, but not at us, as if we were but a bit of Gulfweed in their new-born sight.

One of the many remarkable features of this passage is the way it evokes the security of a domestic scene of nursing mothers calmly attending their young while, at the same time, Ishmael can see the stark contrast of the ferocity of the whale hunt going on unabated beyond the confines of the wall of whales that have hemmed his craft in. It is an ideal passage in its own right to study for clues as to the way great literature can contemplate such extremes and of how some tranquility might be achieved in the midst of urgent times. Ishmael compares the nursery calm with "circle upon circle of consternations and affrights" that surround it and then with himself, also serene "amid the tornadoed Atlantic of my being," nevertheless able to "centrally disport in mute calm" (366). A part of the lesson is surely in Melville's close attention to details of the natural world that show how in the midst of turmoil and confusion a community of whales can still create places of peace and security.

Melville's novel is famous for its gradual build-up of tension as the Pequod and the narrative very slowly approach harpooning proximity to the White Whale. This tension also affects the occupants of the ship including Ahab himself whose character is driven by an obsessive and vengeful need to hunt and kill the whale that took his leg. This character trait is a main engine driving the forward push of the narrative. We have seen that fanfiction works best when brought to bear on character and so I suggest to students an exercise that adapts one of the techniques of fanfiction to the novel's most dramatically drawn character. This is a self inser- tion of oneself in the role of the character in question, Ahab. A good example to start with is one of Ahab's longer speeches such as the one in chapter 118 (entitled "The Quadrant") in which he decries the limited nature of the knowledge that science and technology can provide him (466–467). A quadrant is an instrument that helps to provide an exact reading of latitude by measuring the angle of a celestial body like the sun. Lamentable for Ahab is that it cannot say where he *will* be or, more urgently, the location of Moby Dick.

The point made in this chapter is philosophically interesting as is often the case with Melville. In class, it can be interesting to compare this problem with the uncertainty principle in physics or the fact that it is impossible to know both velocity and position with accuracy. Ahab's predicament cuts to the heart of urgent times when we feel we need the most capacity to make predictions and feel our lack of certain knowledge most sharply. Broader questions regarding the importance during crisis of dealing with the impossibility of absolute certainty can be discussed. To help students come to terms with this, I suggest a *self insertion* exercise in which student readers write themselves into a scene as a new character, or perhaps replace a character. Here, the aim is to discern different actions, options, and outcomes based on the insertion into the narrative of a character with the reader's own moral compass. The passage of interest begins after Ahab uses the quadrant and calculates his latitude:

> Then falling into a moment's reverie, he again looked up towards the sun and murmured to himself: "Thou sea-mark! thou high and mighty Pilot! thou tellest me truly where I *am* – but canst thou cast the least hint where I *shall* be? Or canst thou tell where some other thing besides me is this moment living? Where is Moby Dick? This instant thou must be eyeing him. These eyes of mine look into the very eye that is even now beholding him; aye, and into the eye that is even now equally beholding the objects on the unknown, thither side of thee, thou sun!"
>
> *(466)*

Ahab's speech continues from here with further imprecations against the device that fails to supply him with the knowledge he seeks. Eventually, in rage, he dashes the quadrant to the deck and destroys it. Preliminary to the *self insertion* exercise, it is worth examining the relationship between the words on the page and the character that emerges. These are the rhetorical and other features that will undergo slight or significant alteration in this writing exercise as students place themselves with their own character traits in this fictional world.

Oliver Twist

In my final example, I explore how Paolo Bacigalupi's young adult (YA) novel *Ship Breaker* (2010) renews or de-familiarises Dickens' *Oliver Twist* regarding the role of child labour during the period of Industrialisation. This has been a true eye-opener to my students who discover child labour in the canon as a social ill that always threatens to re-emerge under the pressure of economic hardship. I start with the *5 storyboards* exercise. This means asking students to squeeze the whole of *Oliver Twist* into just five key scenes or storyboards, as if they were preparing to adapt the novel to the screen. I do this to encourage students to synthesise by thinking about what is absolutely essential to know. Each student's five storyboards will also differ greatly from one another and so bring to the surface the durability of the canon based on the varied kinds of attention readers bring to it. It endures because it speaks to so many readers in so many different ways. What's important about this exercise is for students to engage in conversation about why they chose the "scenes" they did. In case students themselves don't select passages from *Oliver Twist* in which the role of child labour during the period of Industrialisation is in focus, it may be useful to home in on chapter 3, for example, which "Relates how Oliver Twist was very near getting a place which would not have been a sinecure" as a key moment in the novel. This chapter can most productively be read in conversation with Paolo Bacigalupi's *Ship Breaker* to illustrate that each energy supply comes with its own system of violence and exploitation. In Dickens' novels it is the coal economy and in Bacigalupi's it is the oil economy that feeds on children's labour.

In order to draw my students' attention to the relationship between energy use and character, I return to the representation of energy questions mentioned above in relation to *Moby Dick* and solarpunk fiction to clarify how this theme is situated within the novel. With that overview, we can look at place in this novel since *Ship Breaker* lends itself very well to a close reading of its setting in relation to energy and its impact on human behaviour and character. By comparing the following three settings in *Ship Breaker* in a *where and what* exercise, students can gain insight into the similarities and differences between an oil economy and renewable energy:

Bright Sands Beach (61–78)
New Orleans II (197–216)
Dauntless (258–316)

Looking at these three settings from the beginning, middle, and ending of the novel, students discuss what happens in these places and what is revealed there. We pay particular attention to Nailer's relationship to these places and how his character develops in different directions depending on the energy system that he is engaged with as a child labourer.

In times of crisis, I find that students need more tools to contrast the doom and gloom of crisis with the narrative means to change the status quo. For that reason, one might consider the voice Dickens creates to disclose the immensely painful scene of human suffering at the beginning of *Oliver Twist*. Have the students do a *define the voice* exercise. Ask them to read closely the first page or two of the novel and guide them to what can be identified as the particularities of this voice. What is the basis of its calm poise, of the sense that it is in control, while it yet discloses a matter of huge emergency: the death of a mother, the tragedy of her life, and the precarious birth of an orphan child? It may well be that for literature to enter the canon, it needs not just to exhibit literary virtuosity in its use of language, it also needs to engage with matters of perennial and profound interest such as Dickens begins his novel. The construction of voice also goes a considerable way towards producing sustained interest and pleasure even if the events told are painful and tragic. This is what it means to be in the hands of a master storyteller.

Students need to be given the confidence to engage with crisis. For Paul Hanstedt this has to do with developing authority in the students by teaching the skills to problem-solve "with deliberation, creativity, resilience, and collaboration" (6). The example of Dickens' first few sentences in *Oliver Twist* speaks as if from a position of safety. It is a voice of resilience and confidence – it might even be regarded as smugly self-satisfied. Arguably, there is a fine balance when narrating human suffering in literary terms that also deliver pleasure to readers. More than one critic has pointed out the ethical problems of Dickens' prose style for entertaining well-off readers with stories of the plight of the very poor. For my purposes, I am not entering the critical debate on Dickens' ethics but rather using his canonical style to teach the strengths of that voice for students in times of crisis. A literary voice can talk about the most painful events, but the poetical and rhetorical aspects of the voice itself can navigate the reader through the turmoil of actual crisis. Embedded in this syntax is some form of human comportment or poise.

So what are the characteristics of this voice? Through a *define the voice* exercise, allow the students to talk among themselves to come up with a few defined attributes of this voice. The aim is to pinpoint the words, phrases, and rhetorical strategies that constitute this engaging voice. Be aware that Dickens is doing (at least) two things – communicating necessary narrative information, *and* performing an authorial personality in subtle and not so subtle ways. You may like to encourage students to consider more broadly some qualities that make for an engaging and interesting voice, be it in verbal conversation or writing. In some respects, a strong narrating presence has qualities we also associate with leadership.

To practise a voice of resilience, teachers could engage in a *ventriloquise the canon* exercise. Ask the students to remember their first problematic work experience. To begin with, they can write it out in their ordinary voice as though narrating it to a friend in a text message or on Snapchat (which by design is perhaps the platform for human exchange with the fewest aspirations to canonicity one can imagine, given that each message vanishes shortly after having been received!). The point is that it will be a style of writing that is of its time and is not striving to speak beyond it. Now, ask the students to return to this initial message with the aim of rewriting it through the previously defined canonical voice of resilience.

This case study has shown how to pair a canonical work of literature with a contemporary YA novel or solarpunk fiction in order to help students understand and above all to participate in what makes the canon endure. I have suggested that key to the resilience of the canon is its continued relevance through the changing historical contexts in which it is read. Of course, apart from relevance, in the canon there is also narrative virtuosity as we have seen in references to Dickens and Melville. It is this combination of literary art and relevance which ensures that readers across generations return to these texts and in doing so take part in the canon's perennial attraction. The teaching activities shown emphasise student engagement in co-producing new knowledge rather than consuming knowledge as in a transmission model of learning. This chapter also promotes a social constructivist approach to learning since readers are invited to see the world as entangled with their own perceptions and capabilities rather than as an independent externality. It's important to remember when teaching the canon to invite students to seek out fellow readers with whom they can discover creativity by resisting, repurposing, or renewing novels that seemed beyond their reach. When students get to participate in these ways in the durability of canonical literature, they take on some of its qualities of resilience and resourcefulness as a bulwark during times of crisis.

Note

1 A current example is: www.fanfiction.net/book/Adventures-of-Huckleberry-Finn/

4

CASE STUDY FOUR

Modern again: tell it from the scars

Texts: *The Turn of the Screw;* "Unnamed Dragonfly Species"; "The Waste Land"; *Poet X*

In the pages that follow, I trace parallels between the responses of authors and poets to crises around the turn of the last century and those of writers today. Henry James' novella, *The Turn of the Screw* (2005[1898]), spans two literary periods: realism and Modernism. It is up to the reader to determine if the ghosts in the governess' account are real as features of a straightforwardly realist story. Otherwise, they may be symptomatic of an undiagnosed psychological problem, though, as the following discussion shows, such symptoms may have real social and historical causes. Such a reading would see the story marking an early stage of Modernism with its exploration of interiority and damaged subjectivity within an overall historically informed account of its times. As such, the story contains many opportunities for learning the skills of interpretation and for seeking evidence for a particular reading.

Even today, *The Turn of the Screw* contains instructive scenes that are helpful when teaching literature in times of crisis. These scenes, I suggest, are born out of the wounds from which twentieth-century Modernism was to grow and they also speak to our times. Thus, in this case study I look at the troubled narrator in the novella by Henry James as well as the speaker in T. S. Eliot's "The Waste Land" in dialogue with contemporary voices such as Juliana Spahr and Elizabeth Acevedo, all of which tell of the scars of Modernist crises, then and now. The aim is to encourage agency in the face of powerlessness, engagement in the face of estrangement. In short, students learn to read fictional texts creatively while developing an understanding of how to live with undecidability in a world that is increasingly difficult to see as a whole. A feature of Modernism is the way it performs a crisis for the reader that evokes awareness of real-world events. There are features of the framing narrative in Henry James' story that do this. For example, it is noteworthy that the possibility of an objective perspective is raised in the framing narrative in the briefly remarked story of the mother waking to witness the same apparition that was presently terrifying to her young son. Objectivity is signalled in this way and then withheld, the crisis is never resolved since the reader is not told whether the ghosts are there for all to see or symptomatic of the governess' dangerous delusions.

When I teach James' story, I admit to both being valid interpretations, namely that there are ghosts in the story and that the governess is psychologically disturbed. That way, I don't validate some students' interpretations over others' and I also invite the students to stay in this moment of crisis with me, a crisis that revolves around indecision and a lack of resolution. Nothing is as it seems, and the reader is invited to "stay with the trouble" (to use Donna Haraway's concept again) by resisting the temptation to come up with the one definitive reading.

The Turn of the Screw

As a Modernist text, *The Turn of the Screw* is ultimately about a system of neglect that sees the lives of vulnerable children in the charge of a woman who may be medically unfit to do her job. Diane Long Hoeveler, in an article in which she shares a metatextual approach to teaching the James story together with Joyce Carol Oates' adaptation of it ("Accursed Inhabitants of the House of Bly" [1992]), calls this system "perverse and corrupt" (119). For Hoeveler,

> that aloof "master," living in splendid isolation in London and untouched by the tragedies occurring in his family, stands finally as a representative of empire; or a clockmaker God; or, most damning of all, the omniscient author who sees all but fails to intervene with a moral or a lesson.
>
> *(119)*

What this approach to *The Turn of the Screw* reveals is that the narrated crisis contains many parts. It is not just about what passes between the governess and her charges in the House of Bly even though that is tragic. The crisis is also associated with the British Empire in India, where the children's grandparents have died without explanation.

Even for contemporary readers, the story contains formal qualities that are helpful when teaching literature in times of crisis. It presents a framing narrative embodying the traditional and trustworthy worldview of realism. At the same time, it shows that narrative form attempting to convey or contain a far more disturbing story nested within it. This nested story is the governess' account and its form is marked by precarity of style and indeterminacy of content. It is either a narrative delivered by a mind oppressed by difficulties rooted in global events, or it is a realist account of an especially tragic haunting. The view of the story as realist is important, I suggest, as a contrasting context for scenes that are born out of the historical trauma from which twentieth-century Modernism was to emerge.

Though the Great War was yet to come, industrialisation had brought with it the exacerbation of class distinctions, the rise of the middle class, and the exhaustion of the colonial system was approaching.

The story's framing narrative indirectly references Empire as it depicts a class of people enjoying affordances traceable at least in part to their privileged status as well as Britain's colonial economic foundations. Among them are city-dwellers and as the guests or owners of a country house they have sufficient leisure time to entertain each other with ghost stories and even to send to the city for a servant to arrange delivery of a particularly delectable narrative. The title of the story comes from this framing narrative in which Douglas, who has sent to the city for the ghost story he plans to share, seeks to arouse interest in it. He suggests that, above and beyond the pleasurable thrills to be derived from a regular ghost story, the one they have discussed involving a child "adds a particular touch" something "charming" (3). He then talks up the story he will present: "If the child gives the effect another turn of the screw, what do you say to *two* children—?" Of the governess' story, we can say that it is symptomatic of the injustices of an uncaring class system and economic imperatives that oblige a young woman to leave her familiar surrounds in order to enter service in the employ of a well to do businessman who wishes to abrogate his familial duties. The framing narrative clearly builds on this and constitutes another "turn of the screw" when the thematisation of children's suffering is said to add to the enjoyment of the tale.

In simple terms, the social and economic background to the governess' crisis is the result of an economy based on exploitation of the global South and within Britain of the class from which the governess comes. As a young woman from the servant class, she must obey the ruling of her employer to manage the fatal consequences of his own family's activities in India. Alone, she must clean up their mess and, after her death, her story also serves the privileged as an entertainment to fill their leisure time. There is some justice in this reading and although it perhaps oversimplifies an even more complex set of social ills it accords with aspects of Jonathan Flatley's work on melancholia and Modernism. Flatley also sees the governess' predicament in terms of inequality at a systemic level. However, this only makes it more difficult to clearly identify causes. Engaging with the ideas of social systems theorist Niklas Luhmann, Flatley points out that a feature of Modernism is the fragmentation of society "in which we live according not to a single logic but to multiple, variable ones" (94). The result of this, Flatley argues, is a shift away from and perceived diminished importance of the local: "Life is less and less determined by local contexts, as the local system context – whether it is the family, the city, medicine, a particular profession, the legal system, or literature itself – is always responding to problems produced somewhere else" (94). Our own times can be understood as the development of this phenomenon seeing as how it is increasingly possible to trace globally distributed causes to any matter or concern we can discern up close.

The crisis produced by this constant shift of responsibility and increasing alienation is expressed at the heart of James' story and is matched by the bipolar emotional shifts of its narrator who begins with enigmatic reference to ups and downs: "I remember the whole beginning as a succession of flights and drops, a little see-saw of the right throbs and the wrong" (20). Even on arriving to take up her duties, the unnamed governess meets a house haunted at least by lingering trauma, unexpressed mourning, and neglect, bringing into it her own symptoms of the wider social ills that pervade the times in which she lives. Our narrator is not blind to this unorthodox situation though she achieves clarity in fits and starts. Thus she concludes her opening chapter veering from thoughts of "a castle of romance inhabited by a rosy sprite" to a grimmer reality:

> Wasn't it just a story-book over which I had fallen a-doze and a-dream? No; it was a big, ugly, antique but convenient house, embodying a few features of a building still older, half-displaced and half-utilized, in which I had the fancy of our being almost as lost as a handful of passengers in a great drifting ship. Well, I was strangely at the helm!
>
> *(24)*

The above references to the house's architecture get to the heart of crisis as a feature of alienation from, and lack of control over, matters presently at hand as well as the destruction of the social fabric, characteristics of the Modernist period well-documented in secondary literature. The house does not present as an integrated whole; instead, it is cobbled together as part old building and part new. And agency over how to direct the affairs of this house cannot be exercised from inside since, "at the helm" of this "great drifting ship" is the governess herself, cut off from the rest of the community including whoever may be considered to be actually in charge of the situation.

Students could be encouraged to consider the architecture of this story as written in the scars of the Modernist tensions arising out of the expansion of Empire, a growing economy, and the distance between the regional and the urban centres. An exercise that works well in this context is the *if walls could speak* writing exercise. Students are instructed to write from the perspective of the house itself in this "drifting ship" of a building using phrases or passages mined from the text that describe or in other ways refer to the house. Students will discover that even though they are on the look-out for something objective in the story, namely the House of Bly as a material thing, they will likely find examples that seem marked by a subjective point of view. This spread of subjectivity is also a feature of crisis whereby a stable, localised self seems to be lacking. Examples of useful passages are, "room by room and secret by secret," "crooked staircases that made me pause," "an old machicolated square tower that made me dizzy" (24), and:

> This tower was one of a pair – square, incongruous, crenelated structures – that were distinguished, for some reason, though I could see little difference, as the new and the old. They flanked opposite ends of the house and were probably architectural absurdities, redeemed in a measure indeed by not being

wholly disengaged nor of a height too pretentious, dating, in their gingerbread antiquity, from a romantic revival that was already a respectable past. I admired them, had fancies about them, for we could all profit in a degree, especially when they loomed through the dusk, by the grandeur of their actual battlements.

(32)

Questions to broaden the focus of the exercise should aim to spread a wide net in looking for significant details. What do the words "crenelated" or "machicolated" mean? To which historical imperatives do such architectural features refer? What does the phrase "gingerbread antiquity" conjure? Nothing seems certain in times of crisis, and yet the challenge is to come up with a reading of the events, if only for the sake of stability. The point here is to unlearn those habits of reading stories on the look-out for individual heroism or failure to be heroic in favour of a systemic approach to reading the big picture.

James' novella is a ghost story with an explicit invitation to its readers to read it as a Modernist tale which contains traces that bear witness to the return of the repressed. Domestic tragedies surround the children: the trauma of dead grandparents in India with whom the children stayed after the death of their military father two years earlier, as well as a deceased manservant and a dead governess. However, there are also the horrors of colonial violence that return in the form of a governess smitten by her employer's display of wealth and class as well as the invitation to become one of his kind:

He was handsome and bold and pleasant, off-hand and gay and kind. He struck her, inevitably, as gallant and splendid, but what took her most of all and gave her the courage she afterwards showed was that he put the whole thing to her as a favour, an obligation he should gratefully incur.

(17)

The governess' tragedy is that she fails to see the ruinous aspect of the upper classes to which she desires to belong. And whether or not they are actual ghosts that appear among the ruins of a country estate to which the children and the governess are banished, they express social and historical wounds that refuse to heal.

When reading this ghost story or any other ghost story in times of crisis, students may wish to consider what else haunts our lives presently. They may likely discuss the idea of the return of the repressed when studying the Modernist novel, or the Victorian, as well as Gothic fiction and horror. Related to that question is the recurring image of ruins, as "not only the physical imprint of the supernatural onto architecture, but also the possessed or deluded people wandering amidst the ruin who fail to see its ruinous aspect," as Tuck and Ree suggest in their glossary of haunting, an account of settler colonial horrors (653). Taking my lead from their glossary, I ask my students to *identify present ruins*. That is to say, "not crumbled Roman columns, or ivy covered abandoned lots," but the present-day state of ruining that we might find within "the quick turnover of buildings, disappearing landmarks, and disposable homes" (653). It is in these places, Tuck and Ree suggest, that we might identify the ruin that "points to the scene of ghost-producing violence" (653). I instruct my students to identify examples of a ruin in their midst, allowing them to interpret these at any point of their becoming a ruin, whether it is at the beginning or towards the end of the process. Who suffers as a result of this process of ruination? Are wrongs being done that now or later could cry out for justice? What action or remedy might the ruin be calling for in this moment that could avert a later return of the repressed? Note that these questions spring from the story. By the time the governess recognises the ghosts in the House of Bly, it is too late to intercept the course of violence that has begun far away from where it now surfaces in its local context.

The Turn of the Screw is the result of many ruins and traces of ghostly violence from near and far. To study this story in times of crisis is to make sense, even if provisionally, out of the many strands of storytelling without simplifying or in any way reading reductively. I prefer, as said, to leave the question of whether the ghosts exist or not open and instead expand students' willingness to identify various expressions of "ghost-producing violence." To do so, I invite students to engage with the spectral fragments of prose through this *estrangement to engagement* exercise. I instruct the students to open their copies of the text at random, maybe on 10–15 moments across the story. They should then pick out a word, or a few words, maybe a phrase, that leaps out at them on those random pages. This could happen at the beginning of a seminar and then, following a discussion about for example the governess as the unreliable narrator of Henry James' story, the students could be invited to structure their random words or phrases taken out of the text into a poem that reflects, however subtly, their reading of the theme or the mood of the story depending on the choice of words available to them. It is important not to let students be guided by a pre-conceived idea of what the story is about so as to allow them some time to sit with uncertainty and proceed out of estrangement into engagement.

"Unnamed Dragonfly Species" and "The Waste Land"

In her "Poetics Statement," Juliana Spahr pays tribute to the influence of the Modernist poet Gertrude Stein on her own poetics (132). Modernist poetics, and especially High Modernism, were arguably a displaced reaction to calamity, registering it symbolically or at several steps removed from the brunt but no less feelingly for that. Thus, Stein's verbal and grammatical experimentation in *Ada* or *Tender Buttons* serves in a direct sense to invoke a crisis in the reader that ostensibly aims to overturn memory or any familiar modes of ordinary description to create the strongest possible connection between expression and things described. But even if this linguistic crisis is an echo of the loss of faith in verbal convention and the shattering of traditional forms of communication, it nevertheless powerfully signifies these concerns.

Juliana Spahr, by comparison, also departs from syntactic conventions in order to bring more attention to environmental calamity and especially climate crisis. The poem "Misanthropocene" is one such example, and "Unnamed Dragonfly Species" from the collection *Well Then There Now* (2011) is another. This long prose poem consists of an account of recent and contemporary humanity, part inventory of behaviour patterns or reactions resulting from or despite the climate crisis. This is formally interrupted by a list of the names of wildlife species of North America many of which are vulnerable or worse according to the International Union for Conservation of Nature's Red List of Threatened Species.[1] The species are alphabetically inserted into the poem, starting with "A Noctuid Moth" (extinct) and ending with "Yellow-breasted Chat." Spahr uses techniques of cutting up and hashing so as to create a species list that is thoroughly entangled with the other poetic lines of the poem, structuring it like a roll call. The pronoun "they" of the poem is not attributed to a defined group but rather refers to a collective human immersion in a problem that also affects many other species similarly:

> They had been alive in 1988. **Eskimo Curlew** They could not even remember thinking at all about the weather that year. **Extra Striped Snaketail** When they really thought about it, they had no memory of any year being any hotter than any other year in general. **Fat Pocketbook** They remembered a few hot summers and a few mild winters but they were more likely to remember certain specific storms like the blizzard of 1976. **Fence Lizard** They did not remember heat as glaciers remember heat, deep in the center, causing cracking or erupting.
>
> *(80)*

Though the individual first person "I" is not used, this doesn't lessen the sense of personal implication for readers thus entangled with the plight of all those referred to by the word "they." The reader is not spared the implied threat of her own extinction since the poet speaks of them in the past tense – "They had been alive in 1988" – implying that they/we are not necessarily alive in the poem's implied future.

Spahr's poem teaches us how to create an inventory that is conscious of the limitations of our perception of the world. The list of species marked in bold interrupts the reading process, giving the reader a choice to either take note of the names of these species, which means losing the flow of the reading, or skipping over them. Students will notice that either choice is an effort, the former because it is disruptive and the latter because it means consciously blocking out the present or impending vulnerability of other species. It is a choice, and it is a meaningful one. Spahr herself says in an interview for *Full Stop Quarterly* that she wishes for her writing to "mean things" and for it to be "more didactic" ("Teaching"). "Unnamed Dragonfly Species" is didactic in its form, not least because that lends itself to creative application to other texts. When I teach Modernism, I put Spahr's poem in dialogue with T. S. Eliot's "The Waste Land" (2015[1922]), a poem that is an evocation of a decimated postwar cultural setting and reflective of a fragmented subjectivity. The final stanza in the first section, "The Burial of the Dead," echoes Spahr's preoccupation with extinction:

> Unreal City,
> Under the brown fog of a winter dawn,
> A crowd flowed over London Bridge, so many,
> I had not thought death had undone so many.

Eliot's speaker reflects on life and death as serious cultural matters by testing the limits and possibilities of memory as a form of requiem for the dead.

The poem figures the difficulty memory faces when crisis and disjunction prevail. It has a bearing on our historical and cultural sensibility. Voices in the poem seem to remember, say they remember, prefer to remember (or forget). In Spahr's poem, by contrast, the speaker's retrospective past tense is produced in counterpoint with a refrain or litany of the names of presently or soon to be endangered species and thus it also speaks from the middle of the calamity. As such, the poem performs a crisis as is often the case in Modernist aesthetics. Its urgency is due to its being composed as the extinctions that the poem reflects are happening at the same time as the poem is being written. The species remain listed alphabetically as data mined from secondary sources online. They have not yet turned into memories, and it is unclear whether they ever will. Because of the struggle with memory and forgetfulness, T. S. Eliot's poem appears more preoccupied with the living than with the dead. The work of remembering is not documented in Spahr's poem. Perhaps this is the reason why "Unnamed Dragonfly Species" sometimes comes across as something that would appear on a monitor in another galaxy thousands of years later. The generic "they" contribute to this, as does the data, marked up in bold.

In this exercise, that I call *report from the future*, I juxtapose these two poems written almost a century apart. The challenges of addressing a crisis such as climate change, especially, but also a pandemic, have in part to do with the conceptual difficulty of comprehending the scale of the processes involved. Yet, a crisis of magnitude needs to be understood as the result of an inter-generational ethical problem that requires solutions across several spatial and temporal scales. In discussing the technique of "Unnamed Dragonfly Species," the students often come away with a sense of how the bolded interjections give a sense of "something being under pressure" and "poking through the cracks" of a narrative. I instruct students to insert interjections into Eliot's poem to form an intertext in the way Spahr does with hers. I ask them to think about the things or activities they treasure now and consider a worthwhile part of their existence. I then instruct them to insert these, in the form of a phrase or a word, into appropriate places. Since the restrictions of Covid-19, this exercise has become an even more profound way of engaging with crisis. The words "writing my diary at my favourite café" now conjure a spectral existence of a world that seems much removed to readers studying under Covid-19 lockdown restrictions.

It has also been shown that the use of lists as a creative writing prompt is a good way for developing the confidence to make the most of one's abilities when for example applying for college. In an article that discusses the need to build student confidence, Jennifer Wells uses a *list and journaling* activity to teach students how to rise above their insecurities regarding their own strengths and abilities when writing college admission essays. An aspect of living with crisis is the inability to see the strengths that one has as well as the many competencies that one is in possession of and that can become useful skills when offered via a compelling narrative. Wells brainstorms possible approaches to the question "How have you taken advantage of the educational opportunities you have had to prepare for college?" She begins by explaining that this question, and many others like it, is not about asking for a list of educational opportunities, but rather "a reflective analysis on how those things had shaped them" (49).

To practise reflecting over what events have taught them, a list is still not a bad starting point. Wells asks students to write two columns, one for their stories and the other for what they say about them. Stories can be anything that comes to mind however seemingly insignificant. An example she gives is how one student describes how she has learned patience from talking to her best friend, who frequently tested her patience (50). Taking inspiration from Wells' work on student writing, I propose that creative writing can suggest ways to connect the immediate with the remote. This is especially important since crisis often creates the sense of being stuck in the present without being able to visualise the light at the end of the tunnel.

The work of memory contributes to creating a path out of the present moment. T. S. Eliot's poem consists of several literary references that are remembered by the speaker of the poem. For example the line, "Those are pearls that were his eyes" which first appears in part I, line 48 recurs, as memory, in part II, line 125, "I remember / Those are pearls that were his eyes." If they don't already recognise the reference, students can be shown that the line comes from Shakespeare's *The Tempest* (Act 1, Scene 2). A well-known writing exercise inspired by Joe Brainard's famous *I Remember* (1975) is to invite the students to write associatively by listing memories one by one, each memory beginning with "I remember." I suggest a creative writing exercise in which students emulate Juliana Spahr's form and intent but via the technique of Brainard's. We first look at the following passage in "Unnamed Dragonfly Species":

> After the piece of the Antarctic Pine Island glacier broke off, they
> could not stop thinking about glaciers and the way they thought
> about glaciers the most was by reading about them on the
> internet late at night, their eyes blurring and their shoulders tight.
> **Hellbender** There they sometimes found argument from the side
> that the oil drillers celebrated, the side that said the melting did
> not matter. **Henry's Elfin** Sometimes, if it was really late at night
> and if they had written on a small notepad beside their computer
> an especially long list of things that were melting as they tended to

do, they would read this argument liked by oil drillers and try to be reassured by the information that if the Antarctic Pine Island glacier melted away it didn't matter much because it would only raise sea levels by a quarter of an inch. **Henslow Sparrow** A quarter of an inch they would think. **Herodias Underwing** A quarter of an inch does not matter. **Hessel's Hairstreak** Then questions would surface through this blurry comfort of small amounts of rising ocean.

(82)

Following a short discussion of this section of the poem, students are then instructed to go online and find out the names of five to six towns on the nearest coast to where they live to complete the exercise *elegiac inventory*. The point here is not that students must know these towns personally, they are likely removed from them emotionally. However, this doesn't mean that they cannot find out a little bit about the towns online. They should then list them in alphabetical order and preface the list with "I remember" followed by something about the towns that they have found online. This exercise can be as creative as the students like since the option here is to expand by inventing a memory associated with that town based on the small amount of information gleaned from a preliminary search online. T. S. Eliot's "The Waste Land" reminds students of the anxieties connected with the process of remembering as implied by the poem's famous opening lines:

April is the cruellest month, breeding
Lilacs out of the dead land, mixing
Memory and desire, stirring
Dull roots with spring rain.
Winter kept us warm, covering
Earth in forgetful snow

In these passages cited above, both Spahr and Eliot are concerned with "blurry comfort" and "forgetful snow," that is with the inattention to or even indifference to the fallout of the Great War, in Eliot's case, and the fatal consequences of climate change, in the case of Spahr. Both poems describe the process of wounds that cannot heal since they are regularly filtered through "blurry comfort" and "forgetful snow." Written a century later, Spahr returns to this wound and therein finds the causes of climate change in the same way her predecessor found causes of the Great War by exposing Western civilisation as being material and decadent and entirely without values. Spahr returns to these concerns, now in the context of climate change, in her poem "Unnamed Dragonfly Species." I compare these two poems because I want to develop in my students the ability to gain perspective via narrative on the profound losses associated with crisis. I share with students the importance of seeing narrative at times as a testament of a crisis survived, as a form of marking or scar that signifies that a wound has healed. This is also as a way of informing students' creative writing endeavours with the potential to heal and develop resilience, as becomes even more apparent when teaching *The Poet X* by Elizabeth Acevedo.

The Poet X

Drawing on the genre of slam poetry, Elizabeth Acevedo's *The Poet X* tells the story of 15-year-old Xiomara Batista who negotiates her relationship to her body, family, and community by writing and performing poetry. Latinx author Acevedo's novel is inspirational and can be incorporated into the literature classroom in times of crisis at moments when forms of resistance are discussed, Modernist or otherwise. I would argue that slam poetry or performance poetry is a contemporary expression of the artistic freedoms we normally associate with the avant garde. Spoken poetry aspires to the quality of *duende*. This Spanish word commonly refers to a high level of virtuosity in performance – often flamenco – that surpasses conventional standards of authenticity and emotional force. The word's Spanish origins are from "dueno de casa" or "due de casa," meaning "possessor of a house" referring to a mischievous spirit inhabiting a house. The term was introduced by the Modernist Andalusian poet and playwright Federico Garcia Lorca in an essay from 1930 titled "Play and Theory of the Duende."

Lorca declares that "every art and in fact every country is capable of duende, angel, and muse" (264), but whereas the muse and angel are external to the artist, *duende* must be roused "in the remotest mansions of the blood" (263). Lorca also emphasises that *duende* cannot be studied:

> there are neither maps nor disciplines to help us find the duende. We only know that he burns the blood like a poultice of broken glass, that he exhausts, that he rejects all the sweet geometry we have learned, that he smashes styles, that he leans on human pain with no consolation.
>
> *(263)*

Nor can *duende* be repeated on command, "any more than do the forms of the sea during a squall" (264). *Duende* has origins as both earth spirit and trickster figure; "The duende, then, is a power, not a work; it is a struggle, not a thought" (263).

This aspect of embodied emotion, and of barely controlled expressive force and struggle, is very much part of slam poetry. In *The Poet X*, Acevedo alludes to the origins of slam in references to boxing when describing Father Sean's past life as a boxer (152) as well as her own eagerness to retaliate when her twin brother gets beaten up because of his sexuality (174). A memorable poetry bout between the poets Ted Berrigan and Anne Waldman in 1979 saw both poets dressed up as boxers and the stage kitted out as a boxing ring (Hoffman 201). Whether Acevedo has this particular historical performance in mind is not clear, but what is clear is the combative nature of slam in the novel. It is important to emphasise though that, despite this, the writing process described in *The Poet X* aims to foster community. The process is one of writing oneself into a sense of security through the ability to share, discover, and celebrate *duende* with others. Xiomara writes, "I learned music can become a bridge / between you and a total stranger" (83) and when teaching poetry especially, that building of bridges, as many literature teachers will attest, begins with the practice of listening. *The Poet X* reminds us how important it is to listen to poetry read out loud and, in a sense, performed.

This aspect of performance reveals a non-combative and more reflective side involving the internal workings of how poetry is received. This is important in the activity of deep listening practised in what Reed Bye calls "Spontaneous 3-Line Poem Practice" in his programme of contemplative pedagogy trainings. In this activity, that I refer to as *voiced poems*, Bye pairs up his students and invites them to create a three-line poem by drawing on "present-moment experience and in response to one's partner."[2] These voiced poems are co-created in the privacy of a corner of the classroom or, sometimes even better, in a breakout room on Zoom. Students experience deep listening when waiting for and then hearing a partner's first line drawn from the present moment. The time this takes can be as long or short as their partner wishes it to be. The response with line two can be as slow in coming but it doesn't have to be. Finally, the initial person rounds it off with a third line in similarly contemplated response to the second. Students can then be invited to share their voiced poems with others in the seminar. These are especially worthwhile during times of crisis as students reach a contemplative moment of peace and concentration when not under pressure to achieve and the only requirement is to share a here and now with another person.

There is a risk when using creative writing exercises in times of crisis that students become too enmeshed in their own stories of grief or frustration. I'm reminded of the importance of a framework for balancing the personal and academic contexts in the classroom. In her work on social justice education, Maurianne Adams emphasises the importance of establishing "an equilibrium between the emotional and cognitive components of the learning process" (15). This resonates with the views of performance artists who do storytelling slams as well and is seen in this word of advice to fledgling storytellers from *The Moth*: "Tell stories from your scars, not your wounds."[3] *The Poet X* contains poems in which Xiomara riffs off the assignments that she gets from her favourite English teacher Ms Galiano. One such assignment instructs students to write about themselves and their achievements as if looking back from a time in the future. Acevedo couples the final two paragraphs of the finished essay with its draft in the form of a poem.

The poem refers to how Xiomara "should be remembered / as always working to become / the warrior she wanted to be" (126). The school essay reads in a much more conventional essay style, mentioning that "Xiomara's accomplishments amounted to several key achievements. She was a writer who went on to create a nonprofit organisation for first-generation teenage girls" (127). When teaching biographical moments in literary texts, I invite students to similarly write from the heart as if at a distance from any hurt or wound they may be dealing with which can be about how they are perceived by others. At the same time, I encourage them to channel their *duende* which, as Lorca might have said, is less about pursuing it than listening for it. This can be done through a *mirror exercise* by inviting students to study themselves in the mirror while creating a self-portrait in words without using the pronoun "I."

The Poet X is a novel that shows readers, especially the young, how to find calm when there is a crisis of meaning. The skill of creating such a space of contemplation can be taught in the literature classroom. I sometimes adapt an exercise called *Am I Saramago*, created by Ursula Le Guin, in which she invites students to write a paragraph without using punctuation on the suggested topic of "A group of people engaged in a hurried or hectic or confused activity, such as a revolution, or the scene of an accident" (18). Le Guin then suggests that the rest of the group reads each other's paragraphs in silence before listening to the author insert their authorial voice that creates the necessary pauses in the text as intended. This sitting with the text without the authorial voice is important. Indeed, Le Guin emphasises elsewhere what she calls the "Rule of Silence" during discussion of any sharing of writing so as to ensure that the author whose work is being critiqued is not "on the defensive, eager to explain, answer, point out – 'Oh, but see, what I meant was...'; 'Oh, I was going to do that in the next draft...'" (134–135, ellipses in the original). This Rule of Silence insists that writing is fully given over to readers for them to engage with and be moved by and to respond. It is a rule worth remembering in this case study about slam poetry which does not explain itself and deep listening that does not ask for more information.

In that *The Poet X* consists of several interlinking narrative strands and episodes, it also actively works on readers' anticipation and ability to connect the dots. In some ways, it is in the spaces between the short poems that the reader's most active participation takes place. A student of mine recalled that in this way it shares similarities with the graphic novel and its use of gutters or the spaces between panels. When reading comics, content in the gutter spaces is important since it does the work of linking the panels together to create a narrative flow. As discussed by Heekyoung Cho, these gutters are given even more creative significance on a digital comic platform such as webtoon. Originating from South Korea and now a very popular comic space with stories also in English, webtoon is a vertical comic strip platform designed for reading on the mobile phone. It expands a reader's digital literacy through its innovative use of gutters that, as Cho notes, "express the duration of time and/or changes of location by its length." This allows comic creators to move parts of the text and the narrative out of the panel into the liminal gutter spaces. Cho also argues that this distribution of narrative information is more effective in the horror genre because webtoons require scrolling down for a vertical display of panels and thus webtoons "accumulate tension by controlling the order of panels that the reader sees."

Webtoons teach us that the author or poet uses graphic and haptic means (e.g. how many thumb scrolls it takes to move to forward) by which to control the speed at which the story unfolds for the reader. It is a technique that can work when retelling the pathway through a crisis. Afterwards, the most difficult passages can be treated as slowly and as carefully as required in order to understand and better share insight. Acevedo's use of white space in her writing can be better understood by paying attention to the popularity of webtoons and their spatial distribution of narrative that migrates across gutters and borders. In this respect, both Acevedo and the webtoon creators shape the narrative on the page. When used in life writing, this is a way of developing the means to turn wounds of the past into marks that are meaningful to others.

In these days of primarily online teaching, I like to suggest ways of bringing the material world into the digital space through the exercise *second firsts*. I invite students to write a passage in an ordinary paragraph form on the topic of their first experience of something. After that, students are invited to reshape it, sculpt, and make something of it that will result in a "second first." This may include spacing, bolding, turning something into a dialogue, repeating and redistributing words, misspelling them, etc. The only restriction is that one is not allowed to insert more material apart from punctuation. Students feel empowered by taking hold of aspects of their life story in this way. The hindsight brought to this second version as well as the creative techniques supplied make this second version also a first.

In this case study I have explored the continuities between the historical ruptures post-Industrial Revolution that brought on early twentieth-century Modernism which, arguably is reprised today a hundred years later, with growing alienation, rise of nationalisms, together with pollution and climate crisis. Strictly speaking, the collection of texts that in this case study falls under the heading "Modern again" also falls under many other headings such as "YA literature" in Acevedo's case or eco-literature in the case of Juliana Spahr's "Unnamed Dragonfly." However, from the point of view of teaching literature in times of crisis, these texts, along with Henry James' ghost story *The Turn of the Screw* and T. S. Eliot's "The Wasteland," are also potent catalysts for students to discover expressions of resilience, adaptation, and self-empowerment.

Notes

1 www.iucnredlist.org/
2 www.naropa.edu/academics/cace/pedagogy-trainings/three-line-poem.php
3 https://themoth.org/

5

WIDER CONTEXTS

Twenty-first-century skills and competencies

Along with the insight that narrative engages readers because it takes them into the midst of crisis (and, as a rule, out the other side) is the realisation that new literary theories are routinely born in crisis. In this chapter I will introduce teachers to the wider theoretical and historical contexts of the kinds of teaching methods shown in the case studies. I will provide an account of recent pedagogical debates and challenges by showing how some education scholars have recently begun to respond to the changes taking place in the twenty-first century by offering radically new teaching methods they consider better suited to our times. Interestingly, literary theory tends to go hand in hand with crisis, as do reading methods. That is to say that radically new ways of reading and working with texts are often as a result of big shifts in the socio-cultural political landscape. Postmodernism, as argued by Fredric Jameson in his seminal *Postmodernism or the Cultural Logic of Late Capitalism*, evolved in response to the rise of the global economy. The impersonal era of big corporations, he argues in this text, gave way to the fragmentation of the subject. By this he means that the human subject has lost the ability to create a sense of continuity between past and future.

Most pertinent for this book, as already mentioned in the Introduction, is Roland Barthes' "The Death of the Author." Written in the thick of revolutionary events of May 1968, Barthes denounces the all-powerful Author-God figure in favour of a reader's response: "The reader is the space on which all the quotations that make up a writing are inscribed without any of them being lost; a text's unity lies not in its origin but in its destination" (148). Barthes' critique of the authority of the author is situated during a period of extreme political turmoil in which it was appropriate for avant-garde intellectuals to define conservative political power in such extreme terms in order to target its injustices. Over the ensuing 50 years, this critique of the hegemonic nature of centralised power has taken a range of forms including Marxism, feminism, and poststructuralism. Recently it has morphed into posthumanism, which is at times the most radical critique of all since it is aimed at the faults it sees as intrinsic to being human while also celebrating the vitality of a life.

Beyond human

Scholars of posthumanism vary greatly in their approaches to the human. The sometimes extreme positions taken up are a measure of what many see as the desperate nature of the environmental crisis facing us. Author of *Posthuman Pedagogies in Practice*, Annouchka Bayley is not the most radical among posthumanist scholars. She urges educators to step outside their comfort zones to meet the challenge of responding to crisis by asking, "What kind of new teaching and learning strategies are we ready to imagine?" ("How Artists Can" 12:40). As Bayley sees it, being equipped to deal with the complexities of today's world requires us humans to think of ourselves as not simply affected by it but as entangled with it – that is, as effective agents integral to the whole (*Posthuman* 141). It is this "being-human, knowing-as-a-human and responding 'humanely' in urgent and troubling times that needs re-imagining," she argues (24). Bayley takes issue with the assumption that "good academic research, teaching and learning is a process that engages with accurately assessing and *reflecting* reality, whilst also simultaneously encouraging students to think *reflexively* about how they do that" (26, emphasis in the original). For Bayley, the task of thinking reflexively is unproductive in today's radically changing world since that approach "operates around the idea that there is some-*thing* that remains still and unchanging long enough to be encountered (by yet another still and unchanging thing/person/observer)" (26, emphasis in the original). I believe this is true in the sense that reality is less an object and more an ongoing process of becoming which, I stress, is amenable to participatory inputs. Far too often, the social sciences are believed to be reflective rather than constructive, as though they need only report on or represent what is happening rather than take part in what that might become. When teaching literature in times of crisis, it is certainly beneficial to stimulate critique and encourage reflection towards problem-solving and care-based learning. Posthumanism emphasises the importance of introducing transformative pedagogical approaches that underscore collaborative communication for envisaging different futures from what seem obviously to be in store.

In lieu of this reflective paradigm, Bayley refers to the "diffractive lens" of posthumanism through which to address a series of setbacks and limitations of the current educational climate, including "the kinds of complexities brought on by enhancements in technology, ecological and environmental changes, globalising forces that trouble simple us/them divides, the reality of living in an evermore [sic] entangled, posthuman world" (20). The term "diffraction" used by Bayley recalls the process used in the study of optics whereby light is passed through a *diffraction grating* to demonstrate its dual nature as both particle and wave. This in turn draws on the original Latin source which refers to fragmentation, the process of breaking into pieces. This sense is central to its use as a riposte to the assumption that knowledge can reflectively mirror the seamless whole of a world. Bayley is inspired by the work of new materialists, especially here by Karen Barad who, in *Meeting the Universe Halfway*, suggests that "whereas the metaphor of reflection reflects the themes of mirroring and sameness, diffraction is marked by patterns of difference" (qtd in Bayley 41).

This preference for the diffractive lens over reflection can be productively incorporated into the literature classroom in times of crisis insofar as it is the basis for participatory teaching methods. Here too in the valorisation of diffraction as a reading method it is possible to see the hauntings of postmodernism and its breaking up of the grand narratives of Modernism. In *The Postmodern Condition*, Lyotard declares the insignificance of grand narratives for scientific discourse, rather "the little narrative [*petit recit*] remains the quintessential form of imaginative invention, most particularly in science" (60). As I hope to have shown in the case studies of this book, it is empowering for students to discover ways of engaging with the world and contributing towards designing the kind of future they imagine for themselves. However, it must also be said that the diffractive lens has its limits since it doesn't change the fact that there is a physical world and with it cultural and socio-economic constraints that we need to put up with.

In their edited collection *Posthumanism and Educational Research* (2015), Snaza and Weaver take what they refer to as "methodocentrism" to task as a form of limited thinking about the world by which "faithfulness to a method is the primary concern of most research" (9). This means that the methods used by researchers have come to replace reality and thereby relegate "most humans, other sentient beings, and non-sentient objects to a subordinate position in which the role of these beings in their own reality and other realities is removed" (9). The claim is sweeping but, again, it is worth knowing of the more radical critiques of pedagogy that serve as a measure of the extreme nature of the crisis that posthumanism is registering. Moreover, what they say does contain more than a grain of truth and suggests caution against adopting too strict an adherence to any given methodology. Snaza and Weaver go so far as to downplay the interactions between a teacher and students, teachers and teachers, as well as students and students because, as they say, there are other experiences happening independent of humans (9).

The case studies in my book push back against some aspects of this kind of thinking that I find impracticable. I would argue that without methods there is no shared reality or basis for communication through which we can come to the important realisations regarding the problem of anthropocentric values and practices, and discuss and disseminate alternatives. Instead of rejecting the methodological means by which understanding can be sought and perspectives expressed, in times of crisis we need to teach our students a multiplicity of worldviews that are mediated by methods and become available through a range of ways of reading. Apart from that, it is worth mentioning that the physical world is itself not method-free. The innumerable life-forms that have arisen and that persevere by reproducing while evolving attest to the fact that there are countless methods even in matter itself.

Another scholar of posthuman pedagogy, already mentioned in the Introduction, Anne Reinertsen, asks for educational practices that are "grounded in immanent interconnections and generative differences: a transversal composition of multiple assemblages, of responsive pedagogues, of inclusion" ("Digital Slow" 148).[1] Following Deleuze and Guattari as well as Isabel Stengers, Reinertsen declares that our task as educators must involve "a willingness to work with uncertainty ... simultaneously resisting conformist pedagogical consensus which may even constrain learning and change" ("Becoming Earth" 4). Reinertsen's influences are posthumanism as well as new materialism which is a distinct though related theoretical emphasis on, broadly speaking, the inherent vitality sometimes seen as agency as well as subjectivity in materiality itself.

A key aim of these theories is to interrogate the central importance of the human subject at the heart of anthropocentrism and this includes a thoroughgoing critique of knowledge insofar as this is often underpinned by the subject–object relation. The relevance of these schools of thought to pedagogy and to the kinds of twenty-first-century skills needed in the literature classroom in times of crisis is potentially substantial since any shifts in the meaning of knowledge itself will impact the way we think about education. Not all new materialist scholars impute subjectivity to matter per se; those who do not still see a subjective side to objects on the assumption that, although for them objects are not subjects, they influence the experience of subjectivity. A familiar example is the digital communication network which comprises countless electronic components, none of which is demonstrably sentient and yet, as a working assemblage, the network has profound impact on the experience and wellbeing of its users. Indeed, some commentators reveal that our means of digital communication are "rewiring" our brains.[2] Even less technically sophisticated objects that are there just to be viewed affect experience in that way.

Jane Bennett views all matter as inherently active and vital and for this reason she accords potentially subjective status to materiality. This is what she means by "vibrant" matter: "a liveliness intrinsic to the materiality of the thing formerly known as an object" (xvi). This is also an assumption that underlies some posthuman theories of matter. A consequence of revising the distinction between object and subject in this way is that the position of the human as the only truly subjective "thing" – with mind, agency, values, culture, etc. – becomes insecure. Some posthuman advocates take more radical positions that are worth knowing about even if only as a way to grasp the level of crisis they see us as facing. Thus, in keeping with Bennett, Bayley, and Reinertsen, but taking their insights and proposals further, Snaza suggests the virtues of what he calls "bewildering education" by which he means a posthuman education that "no longer seeks the production of 'the human' as its end" (40) and that refuses to disclose at the outset what the outcome of education will be (49). For Snaza, education suffers because educators tend to subordinate "pedagogy to a predetermined and predefined goal or endpoint" (49).

Common to all posthuman approaches as well as new materialist ones is the thought that education is a necessary step for rewriting the terms of human engagement with the world and specifically the relationship between humans and non-humans. To revise the status of humanity in this way creates more specifically the conditions for a new valuation of the environment. Some see it as necessary to accord non-living physical things potential or actual subjectivity. What might be more likely and effective would be to go beyond animal rights and human rights and instead talk about the rights of ecosystems or the rights of rivers and lakes, for example, and then to educate our students regarding those rights, in the same way that we educate them about human rights.

Something to bear in mind, however, is that this is not meant to be a new puritanical doctrine of ecological duty that points an accusing finger at humans – at least, not always. Instead, what could be at stake for literature teachers is to make visible the preservation of the best conditions for the joy that is possible for all living things. Bennett and others (including for example Sara Ahmed) believe that revising the status of the human in favour of a more equitable distribution of subjective potential among living and non-living things opens up the possibility for vastly improved experiences of enchantment and wonder for humans and for all life forms as well as the complex material conditions of life. For teachers in times of crisis, one of the most productive lessons to take from these theories is an invitation not to set oneself apart from the meaning-making world, but rather to become part of the self-organising capacity of matter, to join its capacity to crystallise, and to produce sustainable ecologies.

Crisis of the imaginary

Arguably, this destabilising of the distinction between the human and non-human as well as its impact on how we teach is not such a new thing. After all, we often conceive ourselves and the world in active political terms and this has had an influence on how we teach literature, particularly in relation to gender and postcolonial struggles. As Rosi Braidotti notes:

> Women's, gay and lesbian, gender, feminist and queer studies; race, postcolonial and subaltern studies, alongside cultural studies, film, television and media studies; are the prototypes of the radical epistemologies that have voiced the situated knowledges of the dialectical and structural "others" of humanistic "Man."
>
> (38)

Such theoretical frameworks have included a fundamental reconsideration not just of what is on the reading lists in the English departments of the world, but also what the subject matter is, how it's being taught and even who is teaching. To diversify our curriculum, in times of crisis especially, is to challenge power relations and call for deeper thinking about the content of our courses and how we teach them. Preparing students for the future has always been a fundamental stake in education and what is now required of literature teachers perhaps more than others is to enlist the imagination of students in creating that future despite the levels of uncertainty associated with crisis.

Part of the issue is that many standard approaches to education are modelled on what Vanessa Andreotti refers to as a "modern/colonial global imaginary" in which educational institutions "present the concept of the modern nation state as a given (and benevolent) category and elevate it to a place beyond critique" ("Educational Challenges" 102). While Andreotti is writing from within the context of Canadian educational development, much of what she says is relevant also to nations with a less prominent Indigenous history and multilingualism. She notes for example that the way the immigrant experience is taught rests on the host nation producing a "sense of national superiority and benevolence to be sustained" (103). Andreotti refers to "epistemic violence" when referring to the geopolitics of knowledge production and distribution. In times of crisis especially, it is important to be aware of the literature classroom as a highly charged space of knowledge production. With this in mind, Andreotti poses a fundamental educational question: "How can we disarm and de-centre ourselves and displace our desires and cognitive obsessions to wake up to face a plural, undefined world without turning our back to the violences we have so far inflicted upon it?" (109).

Andreotti's work identifies most precisely the kind of entrenched conceptual obstacles higher education innovators face. Her work is most significant as a means of introducing educational institutions to the significance of the radically new world views many contemporary theorists are proposing as well as the historical contexts in which they arise. An important influence on Andreotti's argument is the work of Maldonado-Torres and de Sousa Santos who both refer to the failure of the imaginary as a form of "epistemic blindness to ways of thinking and being outside of modern parameters of intelligibility," referring not to "what modern subjects do not imagine, but to what they cannot imagine" ("Educational Challenges" 104). To those of us who teach literary studies, it is perhaps both heartening and daunting to see that once again it is the imagination that is at the centre of educational development. It falls on teachers of literature to foster that imagination and in times of crisis to keep up with and indeed be ahead of a changing world. A combination of global forces is rapidly shaping our day-to-day lives and education is at the heart of preparing students for uncertain futures. For this reason, it is important that both teachers and students understand the social relevance of their educational programme. The activities outlined in my case studies form the basis of a teaching method that invites students to become co-producers rather than consumers of knowledge. This experience lays the groundwork for students to re-imagine and take part in alternatives instead of accepting whatever is in store, an important skill for learning to engage with crisis.

A large majority of scholars, in literary studies and other disciplines, suggest that the imagination is our most powerful tool for addressing the crises that we are currently facing. For Sardar, this is because it is capable of taking us "from simple reasoned analysis to higher synthesis" and that therefore "the kind of futures we imagine beyond postnormal times would depend on the quality of our imagination" (443). Sardar identifies the challenge as being a matter of developing ways of unleashing "a broad spectrum of imaginations from the rich diversity of human cultures and multiple ways of imagining alternatives to conventional, orthodox ways of being and doing" (443).

Teachers and scholars in the area of environmental education also speak about the imagination as a "source of a revitalized means of promoting the sensual, perceptual and conceptual dimensions of an aesthetic education" (Payne, 305). An "ecopedagogy of imagination," says P. G. Payne, "invokes that which can't normally be accessed, or isn't anticipated, expected and accepted" (306). The imagination can be developed through practising a number of competencies. For guidance, the UNESCO document "Issues and Trends in Education for Sustainable Development" (Lecht et al. 2018) outlines the following competencies as ideally being part of the core of education and, while they are not explicitly linked to the imagination, that faculty is implicit whenever learning from perspectives other than one's own or understanding alternatives to one's own time and place:

- *Anticipatory competency*: the ability to understand and evaluate multiple futures – possible, probable, desirable – and to create one's own visions for the future
- *Normative competency*: the ability to understand and reflect on the norms and values that underlie one's actions
- *Collaborative competency* in the service of participatory problem-solving: the ability to learn from others and to understand and respect their needs, perspectives, and actions; this assumes empathy and empathic leadership, the ability to understand, relate to, and be sensitive to others especially when dealing with conflicts in a group
- *Critical thinking competency*: the ability to question norms, practices, and opinions as well as to reflect on one's own values, perceptions, and actions
- *Self-awareness and cultural awareness competency*: the ability to reflect on one's own role in the local community and global society, which involves continually evaluating and further motivating one's actions

Some of the above competencies are of the kind that one would typically find in the curricula at English departments around the world, others are not. Critical thinking, collaboration, and cultural literacy are to be expected, but anticipatory competency and self-awareness are less frequently discussed in literature classrooms. There are numerous strategies for developing a greater awareness of the role the imagination plays in the literature classroom. In his work on language in the digital age, Kenneth Goldsmith paradoxically instructs his students in the practice of what he calls "uncreative writing" (12), including retyping long sections of their favourite novels, with the goal of teaching them to value creativity (9). Goldsmith also suggests *digitally rearranging texts*. "Words," he reminds us,

> might not only be written to be read but rather to be shared, moved, and manipulated, sometimes by humans, more often by machines, providing us with an extraordinary opportunity to reconsider what writing is and to define new roles for the writer.

> *(15)*

Goldsmith says this makes students aware also of the performative nature of writing: "for many students, they began to view text not only as transparent carriers of meaning but also as opaque objects to be moved around the white space of the page" (203).

Exercises such as these contribute to self-awareness and cultural awareness competency since they draw students' attention to their power as producers of textuality. For example, for *uncreative writing* they are later questioned as to their choice of text and the paratextual devices involved in their retyping, such as the type of paper they chose to print on, as well as the font they used. Unsurprisingly, very few even consider using anything other than Times New Roman (204). In times of crisis, when social media circulates unverifiable information and fake news, it is especially important to empower students with the tools of critical thinking about the role of words as more than "transparent carriers of meaning."

A similar exercise developed by Goldsmith asks students to *transcribe audio files*. None of the resulting "transcriptions" bears any resemblance to any other because how we hear and how this hearing is transcribed into written language is "riddled with subjectivity" (205). We do well as teachers in times of crisis to remind our students of the multiple creative and noncreative ways of working with language since this parallels our digital reality in which information circulates. As Goldsmith recommends, "just think of the way you 'read' the Web: you parse it, sort it, file it, forward it, channel it, tweet it and retweet it. You do more than simply 'read' it" (226).

Goldsmith also suggests ways of disrupting flows of communication to create awareness in the reader of what expression is about. I have adapted one of his exercises which is to ask students to choose words on a page from a text we are studying to be written in *ALL CAPS* to connote shouting (47). This awareness of the material properties of language is sometimes rather confronting to students since it demands their attention in unusual ways. It fosters normative competency since it underscores the norms and values that underlie the action of emphasising, shouting, drawing attention to, as well as being generally emotional or awkward. Another way of drawing attention to the performative aspects of language that also develops collaborative competency is to encourage students to become better listeners. Crisis requires of us to work together in order to problem-solve. The literature classroom can sensitise us to each other through the use of collaborative reading.

As a group, students may for example be instructed to *count one to ten* with one student speaking at a time. If two students say a number simultaneously, the whole group has to start over again. It can be done with sentences from a text or poem if everyone has a copy. This exercise is easier face-to-face but it also works in a digital classroom; then it is of course necessary to pay closer attention to others. At the same time, online collaboration is even more required in times of crisis, as evident during the Covid-19 restrictions, so learning how to hear others is well worth the time. This exercise also has the added benefit of cementing a group at the start of the term. Another such exercise that sensitises students to the performative qualities of language, especially in the digital classroom, is to ask for two volunteers who role play being two very good friends who are having an enormous argument. They may express their heated emotions to each other using vocal sound effects, as well as pauses and the like, but they are restricted to using the words "*I LOVE YOU.*"

Education and emotions

Teaching that cannot engage with crisis becomes an empty gesture unable to impart to students a spirit of independence. Inspired by Paulo Freire's *Pedagogy of the Oppressed* (2000[1970]), Canadian novelist, essayist, and children's author Kyo Maclear is weary of the prevailing paternalism of Western approaches to crisis:

> We are taught that we need a powerful, paternal authority figure in the wake of disaster. It is tough for some people to let go of the idea that we need to be led or we need to lead in moments of uncertainty. Combine this with discourses of the "vulnerable child" and we are deep inside a story we have constructed about our own role and identities as guardians and protectors.
>
> *(101)*

This recalls Naomi Klein's argument in *The Shock Doctrine* (2007) that in fact paternalistic relationships thrive on crises so that they become reinscribed when there is instability, war, terrorist attack, and so on (108). In response to this, Maclear wonders if, in moments of crisis, we can "imagine ourselves adopting the radical posture of an empty hand? Can we hold a space in which to openly listen and bear witness without marching in with an answer?" (101). For Shoshana Felman, crisis and teaching are deeply linked:

> I would venture to propose, today, that teaching in itself, teaching as such, takes place precisely only through a crisis: if teaching does not hit upon some sort of crisis, it does not encounter either the vulnerability or the explosiveness of an (explicit or implicit) critical and unpredictable dimension, it has perhaps *not truly taught*: it has perhaps passed on some facts, passed on some information and some documents, with which the students or the audience – the recipients – can for instance do what people during the occurrence of the Holocaust precisely did with information that kept coming forth but that no one could *recognize*, and that no one could therefore truly *learn, read or put to use*.
>
> *(53, emphasis in the original)*

Felman likens this teaching to psychoanalysis insofar as both "are interested not merely in new information, but, primarily, in the capacity of their recipients to transform themselves in function of the newness of that information." As such, she argues, both psychoanalysis and teaching "are called upon to be *performative*, and not just *cognitive*, insofar as they both strive to produce, and to enable, *change*." Felman's preference for imparting "information that is *dissonant*, and not just *congruent*" with what students already know resonates with Deborah Britzman's emphasis on the importance of difficulty in education, as well as her assumption that psychoanalysis and education have much in common. Well known for her notion of "difficult knowledge," Britzman elaborates her view that education is "an emotional situation and as such, difficult to know" (96).

For Britzman, a sense of our own "incompleteness" is at the scene of instruction and contributes to the difficulty in the form of "conflicts of belief and the capacity to be open to what may, at first glance, feel unbelievable, frustrating, or inaccessible" (100). However, she also maintains that herein lies the capacity for great knowledge and the attempt to avoid this conflict by maintaining that when "pedagogy is unaffected by its emotional situation" this is a lost opportunity to learn (102). Being aware of this aspect of teaching, she suggests, may take some of the pressure off, especially, student teachers who are taught to believe the myth that "everything depends upon the teacher, teachers are self-made, and the teacher must control the students" (103). In actual fact, Britzman argues, these feelings are produced out of emotions that "look suspiciously like anxiety: fear of losing, being lost, lonely, and needing help, and worrying about becoming out of control" (103).

Importantly, it would seem then that the transformative aspect of teaching is not only sought after in the learners but also the teachers themselves. A greater awareness of the emotional aspect of teaching may assist teachers to cope with crisis. In explaining what is sometimes referred to as the "affective turn," Zembylas suggests moving "beyond a reason/emotion binary to an analysis that recognises how emotions become sites of control as well as resistance" (543). Zembylas suggests that "failing to understand how students' emotional attachments are strongly entangled with epistemological, cultural and historical circumstances and material conditions will undermine teachers' pedagogical interventions" (546).

In times of crisis, it is worth taking into account, with Zembylas, that "the desire for empowerment and resistance cannot be taken for granted as a 'natural resource' for critical pedagogy ... rather, the affective tensions around issues of empowerment and resistance must be placed at the heart of critical pedagogy" (546). Embedded in social structures and therefore also in the classroom are, for Zembylas, "bodies and the troubled knowledge they carry" and it is to this we must be attentive in these "(already) discomforting learning spaces" (547). The pedagogical approach will be impacted by this in the bridging of the private and the public in the classroom and towards making legible the non-verbal articulations of emotion in the classroom.

Importantly, acknowledging emotions in the classroom is not only about vocalising antagonism or conflict, even in times of crisis. On the contrary, AnaLouise Keating speaks of "a post-oppositional politics of change," suggesting that the antagonistic argumentative approach used in academic writing and engagement won't properly develop the skills needed today as crisis seems more ubiquitous (*Transformation* 24). Instead she proposes "pedagogies of invitation" that are "nonoppositional and require intellectual humility, flexibility, and an open-mindedness." For Keating, this means offering students stories of our interrelatedness so as to provide "alternatives to the status-quo stories of extreme individualism" (184). Keating advocates what she calls "listening with raw openness" because, as she says, the act of listening "is a crucial yet too often overlooked element in effective class discussions and other forms of dialogue" (196). While listening, Keating says,

> we remind ourselves that each individual we encounter has a specific, highly intricate history, an upbringing and life experiences which we cannot fully know. We don't know the forces that shaped her and, at best, we can only partially ascertain her intentions and desires. Our understanding is always partial and incomplete.
>
> *(196)*

The acceptance of vulnerability and generosity embedded in this approach to listening is especially useful to bear in mind in times of crisis, when we often fall prey to quick solutions and paternalism, as already discussed.

More concretely, this approach translates into a teaching method that is particularly applicable to the literature classroom. Keating explains how she focuses her teaching material around "discussions of commonalities" (*Teaching* 44) as part of her "relational, dialogic approach" (49). She selects a theme and traces it through different texts, "noting the many ways it changes and investigating the socio-cultural, historical, power-laden implications of these alterations" (44). I do something similar in my literature classes when I present the activity *follow the theme*. How far and wide the students track our chosen theme often depends on the course content, but this activity can be adapted for a short analysis looking at one page, a chapter, or a spread of texts, fictional and non-fictional. An example of tracing commonalities that Keating gives is in the comparative reading of Emerson's essay "Self-Reliance," DeLillo's *White Noise*, and Leslie Marmon Silko's *Ceremony*. The questions she poses to her students include: "Compare-contrast Silko's view of nature with Emerson's and DeLillo's. What commonalities, if any, do you find?" (150) as well as "Compare/contrast Tayo's quest [in *Ceremony*] with Jack's quest in *White Noise*: What similarities and differences do you find, and how do you account for them?" Another exercise Keating offers her readers is to trace a theme in material culture outside of the prescribed text on the reading list, for example investigating cook books as well as feminist periodicals searching for gender clues (157).

There is no outside the classroom

Derrida's famous observation in *Of Grammatology* (1976) that "there is nothing outside the text" affirms that texts are always informed by, or implicated or nested within, other texts rather than referring to some grounding non-textual external reality or truth. I believe a similar shift in awareness can be applied to thinking about the role and location of the classroom. Just as a poststructuralist understanding of textuality means that if you step out of one text, you end up in another (or you could be in more than one text at a time), an educator's approach to education recognises multiple scenes of instruction overlapping, intersecting, seguing or adjacent to, or contained within other learning environments, some of which may contradict each other. For example, the education that several family memberships impart is ongoing even during class-time and both of these learning environments coexist with what our peers or tribal groups – online or face-to-face – seek to instil in us. In other words, all situations involve learning about those situations and what other situations permeate or lie beyond them.

The point is that applied knowledge that imaginatively draws on the many other contexts that are presently impinging on or relevant to the official scene of teaching is often the hallmark of a successful literature curriculum. This is perhaps especially true of times of crisis when the ability to see connections across contexts helps develop students' awareness of the "big picture" aspects of their studies. It is certainly important for successful collaborative or inter-disciplinary endeavours. In a discussion paper about how to engage students in the discipline of English literature in a climate where the Internet offers many resources and also competes for our students' attention, Arthur Applebee draws attention to these multiple contexts for learning. Applebee suggests that literary studies can activate students' attention through the act of "Nurturing rich layers of possible links by inviting constant comparison, contrast, and the revisiting of related ideas and experiences" (32). For Applebee, it is also about engaging all students, regardless of ability, by making sure that teaching techniques make use of scaffolding – where learning is built on existing strengths – to ensure the process is student-targeted (33).

For educator Momir Djurovic, we must be more flexible regarding educational needs. Rather than a "just in case" approach, Djurovic advocates "just in time" teaching that "is more about what is needed to know for a certain time, than accumulating knowledge that may never be needed" (137). This is consistent with the importance of maintaining hope within the classroom by treating a range of different futures as in principle possible, especially in times of crisis. An open future, as Maria Ojala insists, is one that is still in the making and, in an important sense, is "impossible to visualize beforehand" (82). I would add that this is not to deny the related idea that a feature of resourcefulness and agency is the capacity to envisage futures and to reach for them. Thus, hope, Ojala notes, can be cultivated "by encouraging trustful relationships and by giving young people the opportunity to concretely work together for change" (82).

Students can be invited to engage with the future in the literature classroom by for example a creative writing exercise in which the speaker addresses the present from the future in a short *letter from the future*. It might let us know aspects of our life today that we can improve as well as what we are already doing well. Perhaps it can evoke simple pleasures from the past that have made a return in this ima-gined future? This kind of exercise works especially well when teaching dystopian fiction regardless of what period it is set in. Such narratives often thematise the "tipping point" that marks a point of no return in relation to a scarce resource or other critical environmental factor. It may be interesting for students to speculate in their letter on what this "tipping point" today might turn out to be. Crisis is often multi-faceted but to engage with it we need to approach it from a particular angle. What aspects of today's society are most at risk of collapse? Where are our current blind spots?

Related to this is the game *the thing from the future*, designed by Stuart Candy and Jeff Watson in 2015 (see http://situationlab.org/wp-content/uploads/2015/10/FUTURETHING_Print-and-Play.pdf). Players are invited to produce a description and sketch (optional) of their thing from the future, and this can be shared with the game-play community using the hashtag #FutureThing. There are four types of future world scenarios the "thing" might come from:

Growth – a future in which "progress" has continued
Collapse – a future in which society as we know it has come apart
Discipline – a future in which order is deliberately coordinated or imposed
Transformation – a future in which a profound historical evolution has occurred

Discoveries made while playing this game will satisfy Applebee's proposal that wider contexts become part of the teaching environment. Ideas will flow from interaction with a widespread online community and these can feed back into the *letter from the future*.

For some teachers, these ways of engaging with crisis in the literature classroom may include aspects of activism. For Elizabeth Ammons in *Brave New Words: How Literature Will Save the Planet*, the problem with humanist discourse is its heavy focus on critique perpetuated via literary studies often to the exclusion of a more balanced interest in the positives along with negatives. Ammons stresses that "If we do not include answers alongside critiques, hope alongside anger, and activism alongside discourse and *talk about both terms* in each of these pairs, what is the point?" (12, emphasis in the original). For Ammons, the value of the humanities "resides in the power of words to inspire us, to transform us, to give us strength and courage for the difficult task of *re*-creating the world" (14, emphasis in the original). These would be the conditions for encountering a "threshold concept," which has a "potential effect on student learning and behaviour ... to occasion a significant shift in the perception of a subject, or part thereof" (Meyer and Land 4). A transformative perspective, by comparison, "is likely to involve an affective component – a shift in values, feeling or attitude" (7).

No matter how we acknowledge the world or worlds outside it, the classroom itself is a place of engagement with that multiple set of contexts understood themselves to be often very different and at times confusing or chaotic learning environments. This means rather than learning *about* literary forms as though they all occur within a single world, students learn *with* them to understand how different forms of expression constitute different worlds. It means doing things with students, rather than for them.

Above all, the classroom is a place of listening for the voices telling of the outside even when they are also in the room.

Teachers are also obliged to hear other voices, though it is important for them not to become overwhelmed with new information. As we have seen in this chapter, I have drawn on many other pedagogues and theorists for the valuable insights on teaching through troubling times they offer. As I draw the chapter to an end, having referred to many other experts I want to remind teachers that their own experience and enthusiasm are equally precious to their students. Just as bell hooks cautions that "many students have difficulty taking seriously what they themselves have to say because they are convinced that the only person who says anything of note is the teacher" (150), so the same can be said regarding the relationship between teachers and theorists.

There are as many approaches to teaching as there are teachers. There are many teachers out there with little knowledge of theoretical readings in the area of pedagogy. However, this doesn't mean that what those teachers have to say is not worth listening to. By this I mean that one of the most efficient ways of finding the professional support needed in times of crisis is to take avail of your colleagues' experience. This could mean establishing an online teachers' café where teachers get to swap ideas and stories about their teaching experience in and outside the classroom. Everyone benefits when we listen to each other, including and, most importantly, our students.

Notes

1 I reproduce Reinertsen's own footnote in full: "Many sentences in this article might appear abrupt and incomplete. Grammatical rules are challenged. I write messy. I write messy texts. This is deliberate and part of my plea for openness and newness, to escape the legacy of the *linguistic turn* in science and research and the discursive certainties that are created through it. Creating new words and word assemblies is part of my plea. Inquiry as pedagogy as constant change needs concepts and genres that are indirect and vibrating with potentialities, not positivist representation. *Cesi n'est pas une pipe* (Wikipedia, 2020a)."

2 Authors such as Nicholas Carr, *The Shallows: How the Internet is Changing the Way We Think, Read and Remember* (2010) and *The Glass Cage: How Our Computers are Changing Us* (2015), and Susan Greenfield, *Mind Change: How Digital Technologies are Leaving Their Mark* (2015).

BIBLIOGRAPHY

Acevedo, Elizabeth. *The Poet X*. HarperTeen, 2018.

Adams, Maurianne. "Pedagogical Frameworks for Social Justice Education." *Teaching for Diversity and Social Justice*, edited by Maurianne Adams, Lee Anne Bell, and Patt Griffin. Routledge, 2007, pp. 15–33.

Ammons, Elizabeth. *Brave New Words: How Literature Will Save the Planet*. University of Iowa Press, 2010.

Andreotti, Vanessa de Oliveira. "The Educational Challenges of Imagining the World Differently." *Canadian Journal of Development Studies / Revue canadienne d'études du développement*, vol. 37, no. 1, 2016, pp. 101–112.

Andreotti, Vanessa de Oliveira and Lynn Mario T. M. de Souza. *Learning to Read the World Through Other Eyes*. Global Education Derby, 2007.

Anwaruddin, Sardar M. "Why Critical Literacy should Turn to 'the Affective Turn': Making a Case for Critical Affective Literacy." *Discourse: Studies in the Cultural Politics of Education*, vol. 37, no. 3, 2015, pp. 381–396.

Applebee, Arthur. "Engaging Students in the Disciplines of English: What are Effective Schools Doing?" *The English Journal*, vol. 91, no. 6, 2002, pp. 30–36.

Arao, Brian and Kristi Clemens. "From Safe Spaces to Brave Spaces: A New Way to Frame Dialogue Around Diversity and Social Justice." *The Art of Effective Facilitation: Reflections from Social Justice Educators*, edited by Lisa M. Landreman. Stylus Publishing, 2013, pp. 135–150.

Bacigalupi, Paolo. *Ship Breaker*. Little, Brown Book Group, 2010.

Barnacle, Robyn and Gloria Dall'Alba. "Committed to Learn: Student Engagement and Care in Higher Education." *Higher Education Research and Development*, vol. 36, no. 7, 2017, pp. 1326–1338.

Barthes, Roland. "The Death of the Author." *Image – Music – Text*, translated by Stephen Heath, Farrar, Straus and Giroux, 1977, pp. 142–148.

Bayley, Annouchka. "How Artists Can Improve Educational Excellence." November 2016 in Leamington Spa, UK. TEDx Talks video, 13:16, 2017. https://www.youtube.com/wa tch?v=bMI6cFF5XfY.

Bayley, Annouchka. *Posthuman Pedagogies in Practice: Arts Based Approaches for Developing Participatory Futures*. Palgrave Macmillan, 2018.

Bennett, Jane. *Vibrant Matter: A Political Ecology of Things*. Duke University Press, 2010.

Benson, Josef. *J. D. Salinger's The Catcher in the Rye: A Cultural History*. Rowman & Littlefield, 2018.

Bonnett, Michael. "Schools as Places of Unselving: An Educational Pathology?" *Exploring Education through Phenomenology: Diverse Approaches*, edited by G. Dall'Alba. Wiley-Blackwell, 2009, pp. 28–40.

Bonus, Rick. *The Ocean in the School: Pacific Islander Students Transforming Their University*. Duke University Press, 2020.

Borrego, Maura, Elliot P. Douglas, and Catherine T. Amelink. "Quantative, Qualitative, and Mixed Research Methods in Engineering Education." *Journal of Engineering Education*, vol. 98, no. 1, January 2009, pp. 53–66.

Botstein, Leon. "Redeeming the Liberal Arts." *Liberal Education*, vol. 104, no. 4, Fall 2018, pp. 74–79.

Boucher, Abigail, Chloe Harrison, and Marcello Giovanelli. "How Reading Habits have Changed During the Covid-19 Lockdown." *The Conversation*, 5 October 2020. https://theconversation.com/how-reading-habits-have-changed-during-the-covid-19-lockdown-146894.

Braidotti, Rosi. "A Theoretical Framework for the Critical Posthumanities." *Theory, Culture & Society*, vol. 36, no. 6, 2019, pp. 31–61.

Brainard, Joe. *I Remember*. Full Court Press, 1975.

Brennan, Teresa. *The Transmission of Affect*. Cornell University Press, 2004.

Britzman, Deborah P. "Between Psychoanalysis and Pedagogy: Scenes of Rapprochement and Alienation." *Curriculum Inquiry*, vol. 43, no. 1, 2013, pp. 95–117. doi:10.1111/curi.12007.

Brooke, Robert. "Underlife and Writing Instruction." *On Writing Research: The Braddock Essays 1975–1988*, edited by Lisa Ede. Bedford St. Martin's, 1999, pp. 229–241.

Butler, Octavia E. *Parable of the Sower*. 1993. Open Road Media, 2000. ProQuest Ebook Central. ebookcentral.proquest.com/lib/uu/reader.action?docID=1803491.

Bye, Reed. "Spontaneous 3-Line Poem Practice." Naropa University. https://www.naropa.edu/academics/cace/pedagogy-trainings/three-line-poem.php.

Carmen, Karen. "Song of Solomon." *Critical Insights Toni Morrison*, edited by Solomon O. Lyasere and Marla W. Lyasere. Salem Press, 2012, pp. 96–116.

Carr, Nicholas. *The Glass Cage: How Our Computers Are Changing Us*. W. W. Norton & Company, 2015.

Carr, Nicholas. *The Shallows: How the Internet Is Changing the Way We Think, Read and Remember*. Atlantic Books, 2010.

Carroll, Lewis. *Alice's Adventures in Wonderland*. 1865. VolumeOne Publishing, 1998. https://www.adobe.com/be_en/active-use/pdf/Alice_in_Wonderland.pdf.

Cho, Heekyoung. "The Webtoon: A New Form for Graphic Narrative." *The Comic Journal*, 18 July 2016. www.tcj.com/the-webtoon-a-new-form-for-graphic-narrative/.

Clough, Patricia. "Introduction." *The Affective Turn: Theorizing the Social*, edited by P. Clough and J. Halley. Duke University Press, 2007, pp. 1–33.

Collins, Suzanne. *The Hunger Games*. Scholastic Corporation, 2008.

Cook-Sather, A., C. Bovill, and P. Felten. *Engaging Students as Partners in Teaching and Learning: A Guide for Faculty*. Jossey-Bass, 2014.

Cooper, Karyn and Robert White. *Democracy and Its Discontents: Critical Literacy Across Global Contexts*. Sense Publishers, 2015.

Coppa, Francesca. *The Fanfiction Reader: Folk Talks for The Digital Age*. University of Michigan Press, 2017.

Costa, Rosa and Iris Mendel. "Feminist Science Literacy as a Political and Pedagogical Challenge: Insights from a High School Research Project." *Teaching Gender: Feminist Pedagogy and Responsibility in Times of Political Crisis*, edited by Beatriz Revelles-Benavente and Ana M. González Ramos. Routledge, 2017, pp. 81–98. doi:10.4324/9781315204161.

Cubitt, Sean. *Finite Media: Environmental Implications of Digital Technologies*. Duke University Press, 2017.

Damasio, Antonio R. *The Feeling of What Happens: Body, Emotion and the Making of Consciousness*. Heinemann, 1999.

Dannenberg, Sascha and Theresa Grapentin. "Education for Sustainable Development – Learning for Transformation. The Example of Germany." *Journal of Futures Studies*, vol. 20, no. 3, March 2016, pp. 7–20. doi:10.6531/JFS.2016.20(3).A7.

Dassow, Laura Walls. "Beyond Representation: Deliberate Reading in a Panarchic World." *Post-Digital: Dialogues and Debates from Electronic Book Review* vol. 1, edited by Joseph Tabbi. Bloomsbury Academic, 2020, pp. 327–334.

Davidson, Cathy N. *The New Education: How to Revolutionize the University to Prepare Students for a World in Flux*. Basic Books, 2017.

Derrida, Jacques. *Of Grammatology*. Johns Hopkins University Press, 1976.

Djurovic, Momir. *Higher Education and Small Countries*. Proceedings, Future Education: Effective Learning in an Age of Increasing Speed, Complexity and Uncertainty, Rome, 2017, pp. 137–140.

Eliot, T. S. *"The Wasteland." The Poems of T. S. Eliot Volume 1 Collected and Uncollected Poems*, edited by Christopher Ricks and Jim McCue. Faber & Faber, 2015, pp. 54–71.

Felman, Shoshana. "Education and Crisis, or the Vicissitudes of Teaching." *Testimony: Crises of Witnessing in Literature, Psychoanalysis and History*, edited by Shoshana Felman and Dori Laub. Routledge, 1992, pp. 1–57.

Field, Kelly. "10 Tips to Support Students in a Stressful Shift to Online Learning. Coping With Coronavirus," *Chronicle of Higher Education*, 2020, pp. 8–11.

Flatley, Jonathan. "Reading into Henry James: Allegories of the Will to Know in *The Turn of the Screw*." *Affective Mapping: Melancholia and the Politics of Modernism*, Harvard University Press, 2008, pp. 85–104.

Foucault, Michel. "The Masked Philosopher." *The Essential Works of Foucault, 1954–1984, vol. 1, Ethics: Subjectivity and Truth*, edited by Paul Rabinow. New Press, 1997, pp. 321–328.

Freire, Paulo. *Pedagogy of the Oppressed*. 1970. Continuum, 2000.

Giroux, Henry. "Educated Hope in Dark Times: The Challenge of the Educator/Artist as a Public Intellectual." *ArtsEverywhere What Education Do We Need?*, edited by Jaroslav Andel and Henry Giroux, 20 March 2018. https://artseverywhere.ca/2018/03/20/education-dem ocracy/?fbclid=IwAR24kB7D96QxjSB5Sai5EARovFdnEQURlN8-SX6OmIC1w2SMM xOuX3b9ZE4.

Giroux, Henry. "When Schools Become Dead Zones of the Imagination: A Critical Pedagogy Manifesto." *Policy Futures in Education*, vol. 12, no. 4, 2014, pp. 491–499.

Global Footprint Network. Advancing the Science of Sustainability. https://www.footprint network.org/.

Goldsmith, Kenneth. *Uncreative Writing: Managing Language in the Digital Age*. Columbia University Press, 2011.

Grahame, Jenny and Kate Oliver. *The Hunger Games: An EMC Study Guide*. English and Media Centre, 2013.

Greenfield, Susan. *Mind Change: How Digital Technologies Are Leaving Their Mark*. Random House, 2015.

Haan, Gerhard de. "The Development of ESD-Related Competencies in Supportive Institutional Frameworks." *International Review of Education*, vol. 56, no. 2–3, 2010, pp. 315–328.

Haidt, Jonathan and Greg Lukiano. *The Coddling of the American Mind*. Penguin Books, 2018.

Hanstedt, Paul. *Creating Wicked Students: Designing Courses for a Complex World*. Stylus Publishing, 2018.

Haraway, Donna. *Staying With the Trouble: Making Kin in the Chthulucene*. Duke University Press, 2016.

Haraway, Donna. *When Species Meet*. University of Minnesota Press, 2008.

Hillis, David M. *Laboratory of David M. Hillis*. http://www.zo.utexas.edu/faculty/antisense/index.html.

Hoeveler, Diane. "Teaching *The Turn of the Screw* Metatextually." *Approaches to Teaching Henry James's Daisy Miller and The Turn of the Screw*, edited by Kimberly C. Reed and Peter G. Beidler. MLA, 2005, pp. 118–124.

Hoffman, Tyler. *American Poetry in Performance from Walt Whitman to Hip Hop*. The University of Michigan Press, 2011.

hooks, bell. *Teaching to Transgress*. Routledge, 1994.

Ishiguro, Kazuo. *Never Let Me Go*. Faber & Faber, 2005.

IUCN. International Union for Conservation of Nature's Red List of Threatened Species. https://www.iucnredlist.org/, 2021.

James, Henry. *The Turn of the Screw*. 1898. Giunti, 2005.

Jameson, Fredric. *Postmodernism, Or the Cultural Logic of Late Capitalism*. Duke University Press, 1991.

Jamison, Anne Elizabeth. *Why Fanfiction Is Taking Over the World*. Smart Pop, 2013.

Janks, Hilary. "Critical Literacy's Ongoing Importance for Education." *Journal of Adolescent and Adult Literacy*, vol. 57, no. 5, 2014, pp. 349–356.

Janks, Hilary. *Literacy and Power*. Routledge, 2010.

Kagawa, F. and David Selby. "Climate Change Education: A Critical Agenda for Interesting Times." *Education and Climate Change: Living and Learning in Interesting Times*, edited by F. Kagawa and D. Selby. Routledge, 2010, pp. 241–243.

Kagawa, F. and D. Selby, editors. *Education and Climate Change: Living and Learning in Interesting Times*. Routledge, 2010.

Kazan, Tina S. "Dancing Bodies in the Classroom: Moving Toward an Embodied Pedagogy." *Pedagogy*, vol. 5, no. 3, 2005, pp. 379–408.

Keating, AnaLouise. *Teaching Transformation: Transcultural Classroom Dialogues*. Palgrave Macmillan, 2007.

Keating, AnaLouise. *Transformation Now! Toward a Post-Oppositional Politics of Change*. University of Illinois Press, 2013.

Kilo What? http://kilowh.at/.

Klein, Naomi. *The Shock Doctrine*. Random House of Canada, 2007.

Ko, Susan. *Teaching Online: A Practical Guide*, 4th edition. Taylor & Francis, 2017.

Lambert, J. *Digital Storytelling: Capturing Lives, Creating Community*. Digital Diner Press, 2002.

Langer, Judith. *Envisioning Knowledge: Building Literacy in the Academic Disciplines*. Teachers College Press, 2011.

Langer, Judith. "Rethinking Literature Instruction." *Literature Instruction: A Focus on Student Response*, edited by J. Langer. NCTE, 1992.

Lave, Jean and Etienne Wenger. *Situated Learning: Legitimate Peripheral Participation*. Cambridge University Press, 1991.

Le Guin, Ursula K. *Steering the Craft: A 21st-Century Guide to Sailing the Sea of Story*. First Mariner Books, 2015.

Lecht, A., J. Heiss, and W. J. Byun, editors. "Issues and Trends in Education for Sustainable Development." UNESCO Publishing, 2018.

Levinas, Emmanuel. *Otherwise than Being or Beyond Essence*. Translated by Alphonso Lingis. Springer Science+Business Media, 1991.

Lorca, Federico Garcia. "From Play and Theory of the Duende." 1930. Translated by Christopher Maurer. *Twentieth Century Theatre: A Sourcebook*, edited by Richard Drain. Routledge, 2002, pp. 263–265.

Lyotard, Jean François. *The Postmodern Condition: a Report on Knowledge*. 1984. Manchester University Press, 2004.

Maclear, Kyo. "Pedagogy of an Empty Hand: What Are the Goods of Education? What Is Teaching Good for?" *Curriculum Inquiry*, vol. 46, no. 1, 2016, pp. 98–109.

Maldonado-Torres, N. "The Topology of Being and the Geopolitics of Knowledge: Modernity, Empire, Coloniality 1." *City*, vol. 8, no. 1, 2004, pp. 29–56.

Melville, Herman. *Moby Dick or The White Whale*. 1851. The St. Botolph Society, 1922.

Meyer, Jan and Ray Land. "Threshold Concepts and Troublesome Knowledge: Linkages to Ways of Thinking and Practising within the Disciplines." *Enhancing Teaching-Learning Environments in Undergraduate Course, Occasional Report*, 4, May 2003, pp. 1–12. www.researchgate.net/publication/285473047_Threshold_concepts_and_troublesome_knowledge_Linkages_to_ways_of_thinking_and_practising_within_the_disciplines.

Milne, Markus J., Kate Kearins, and Sara Walton, "Creating Adventures in Wonderland: The Journey Metaphor and Environmental Sustainability." *Organization*, vol. 13, no. 6, 2006, pp. 801–839.

Morris, Sean Michael. "Fostering Care and Community at a Distance." www.seanmichaelmorris.com, 28 May 2020.

Morrison, Toni. *Song of Solomon*. A Plume Book, 1987.

Morton, Timothy. *Hyperobjects: Philosophy and Ecology after the End of the World*. University of Minnesota Press, 2013.

Mueller, Derek N. "Digital Underlife in the Networked Writing Classroom." *Computers and Composition* 26, 2009, pp. 240–250.

Nixon, Rob. *Slow Violence and the Environmentalism of the Poor*. Harvard University Press, 2013.

Noble, Safiya Umoja. *Algorithms of Oppression: How Search Engines Reinforce Racism*. New York University Press, 2018.

Ojala, Maria. "Hope and Anticipation in Education for a Sustainable Future." *Futures*, vol. 94, November 2017, pp. 76–84. https://doi.org/10.1016/j.futures.2016.10.004.

Orr, David W. "What Is Education For?" 1990. *Hope Is an Imperative*, Island Press, 2011, pp. 237–245. doi:10.5822/978-971-61091-61017-0_24.

Paulson, William. *Literary Culture in a World Transformed: A Future for the Humanities*. Cornell University Press, 2001.

Payne, Phillip G. "Remarkable-Tracking, Experiential Education of the Ecological Imagination." *Environmental Education Research*, vol. 16, no. 3–4, 2010, pp. 295–310.

Perloff, Marjorie, *Differentials: Poetry, Poetics, Pedagogy*. University of Alabama Press, 2004.

Ray, Sarah Jaquette. *A Field Guide to Climate Anxiety: How to Keep You Cool on a Warming Planet*. University of California Press, 2020.

Reinertsen, Anne. "Becoming Earth." *Becoming Earth: A Post Human Turn in Educational Discourse Collapsing Nature/Culture Divides*, edited by Anne Reinertsen. Sense Publishers, 2016, pp. 1–14.

Reinertsen, Anne. "Digital Slow: Brahmanism, Zetetic Wild Sciences, and Pedagogics." *Critical Studies in Teaching and Learning*, vol. 8, 2020, pp. 146–167.

Revelles-Benavente, Beatriz and Ana M. González Ramos, editors. *Teaching Gender: Feminist Pedagogy and Responsbility in Times of Political Crisis*. Routledge, 2017.

Ribeiro, Sandra P. M., Antonia A. F. G. Moreira, Cristina M. F. Pinto da Silva, "Digital Storytelling: Emotions in Higher Education." *Competencies in Teaching, Learning, and Educational Leadership in the Digital Age*, edited by J. M. Spector, Dirk Ifenthaler, Demetrios G. Sampson, and Pedro Isaias. Springer International Publishing, 2016, pp. 149–167.

Richardson, Judith. "A Conversation with Jay McTighe." *Principal Leadership*, September 2008, pp. 30–34.

Ricoeur, Paul and Matthew Escobar. "Otherwise: A Reading of Emmanuel Levinas's *Otherwise than Being or beyond Essence*." *Yale French Studies*, no. 104, 2004, Encounters with Levinas. Yale University Press, pp. 82–99.

Rigby, Kate. "Contact Improvisation: Dance with the Earth Body You Have." *Manifesto for Living in the Anthropocene*, edited by Katherine Gibson, Deborah Bird Rose, and Ruth Fincher. Punctum Books, 2015, pp. 44–48.

Rogowska-Stangret, Monika. "Sharing Vulnerabilities: Searching for 'Unruly Edges' in Times of the Neoliberal Academy." *Teaching Gender*, edited by Beatriz Revelles-Benavente and Ana M. González Ramos. Routledge, pp. 11–24.

Rose, Deborah Bird. *Reports from a Wild Country: Ethics for Decolonisation*. University of New South Wales Press, 2004.

Rosenblatt, L. M. "A Performing Art." *The English Journal*, November 1966, vol. 55, no. 8, pp. 999–1005.

Rossman, Jennifer Lee. "Riot of the Wind and Sun." *Glass and Gardens: Solarpunk Summers*, edited by Sarena Ulibarri. World Weaver Press, 2018, pp. 24–39.

Rubin, Anita. "Hidden, Inconsistent, and Influential: Images of the Future in Changing Times." *Futures*, vol. 45, January 2013, pp. 38–44. doi:10.1016/j.futures.2012.11.011.

Salinger, J. D. *The Catcher in the Rye*, 1951. Little Brown and Company, 2019.

Sandvoss, Cornel. *The Death of the Reader? Literary Theory and the Study of Texts in Popular Culture. The Fan Fiction Studies Reader*, edited by Karen Hellekson and Kristina Busse. University of Iowa Press, 2014.

Sardar, Ziauddin. "Welcome to Postnormal Times." *Futures*, vol. 42, no. 5, June 2010, pp. 435–444.

Sedgwick, Eve Kosofsky. "Queer and Now." *Tendencies*. Routledge, 1994, pp. 1–20.

Shelley, Mary Wollstonecraft. *Frankenstein; or, The Modern Prometheus*. Penguin Classics, 2013.

Siddiqui, Jamila R. "Restyling the Humanities Curriculum of Higher Education for Posthuman Times." *Curriculum Inquiry*, vol. 46, no. 1, 2016, pp. 62–78.

Snaza, Nathan. "Bewildering Education." *Journal of Curriculum and Pedagogy*, vol. 10, no. 1, 2013, pp. 38–54. doi:10.1080/15505170.2013.783889.

Snaza, Nathan and John A. Weaver, editors. *Posthumanism and Educational Research*. Routledge, 2015.

Sousa Santos, Boaventura de. "Beyond Abyssal Thinking: From Global Lines to Ecologies of Knowledges." *Review (Fernand Braudel Center)*, vol. 30, no. 1, 2007, pp. 45–89. https://www.jstor.org/stable/40241677.

Spahr, Juliana. "Poetics Statement." *American Poets in the 21st Century: The New Poetics*, edited by Claudia Rankine and Lisa Sewell. Weslyan University Press, 2007, pp. 131–133.

Spahr, Juliana. "Teaching in the Margins: Juliana Spahr." *Full Stop Quarterly*, 29 November 2012, www.full-stop.net/2012/11/29/features/the-editors/teaching-in-the-margins-juliana-spahr/.

Spahr, Juliana. *Well Then There Now*. David R. Godine, 2011.

Terranova, Fabrizio, director. *Donna Haraway: Story Telling for Earthly Survival*. 2016.

Tuck, Eve and C. Ree. "A Glossary of Haunting." *Handbook of Autoethnography*, edited by Stacey Holman Jones, Tony E. Adams, and Carolyn Ellis. Left Coast Press, 2013, pp. 639–658.

Turner, Jennifer D. and Autumn Griffin. "Power, Language, and Social Change: A Dialogue with Hilary Janks about Critical Literacy in a Post-Truth World." *Language Arts*, vol. 96, no. 5, 2019, pp. 318–324.

Twain, Mark. *The Adventures of Huckleberry Finn (Tom Sawyer's Comrade)*. 1884. A Glassbook Classic.

Twain, Mark. *Mark Twain's Adventures of Tom Sawyer and Huckleberry Finn*, edited by Alan Gribben. NewSouth Books, 2011.

Uhl, Christopher. *Developing Ecological Consciousness: The End of Separation*. Rowman and Littlefield Publishers, 2003.

VanderMeer, Jeff. *Annihiliation*. Fourth Estate, 2014.

VanderMeer, Jeff. "From Annihilation to Acceptance: A Writer's Surreal Journey." *The Atlantic*, 28 January 2015. https://www.theatlantic.com/entertainment/archive/2015/01/from-annihilation-to-acceptance-a-writers-surreal-journey/384884/.

Wals, Arjen E. J. "Beyond Reasonable Doubt: Education and Learning for Socio-Ecological Sustainability in the Anthropocene." Inaugural Address, Wageningen University, 17 December 2015. edepot.wur.nl/365312

Wells, Jennifer. "'It Sounds like Me': Using Creative Nonfiction to Teach College Admissions Essays." *The English Journal*, vol. 28, no. 1, 2008, pp. 47–52.

Wiggins, Grant and Jay McTighe, "Examining the Teaching Life." *Educational Leadership*, vol. 63, no. 6, 2006, pp. 26–29.

Wiggins, Grant and Jay McTighe, *Understanding by Design*. Association for Supervision and Curriculum Development, 2005.

Williams, Bronwyn T. "'Tomorrow Will Not Be Like Today': Literacy and Identity in a World of Multiliteracies." *Journal of Adolescent & Adult Literacy*, vol. 51, no. 8, May 2008, pp. 682–686.

Woodson, Jacqueline. *Brown Girl Dreaming*. Puffin Books, 2016.

Worley, Peter. *The If Machine: Philosophical Enquiry in the Classroom*. Bloomsbury Publishing, 2010.

Yaeger, Patricia. "Editor's Column: Literatures in the Ages of Wood, Tallow, Coal, Whale Oil, Gasoline, Atomic Power, and Other Energy Sources." *PMLA*, vol. 126, no. 2. 2011, pp. 305–310.

Young, Michael, "Overcoming the Crisis in Curriculum Theory: A Knowledge-Based Approach." *Journal of Curriculum Studies*, vol. 45, no. 2, 2013, pp. 101–118. doi:10.1080/00220272.2013.764505.

Zembylas, Michalinos. *Emotion and Traumatic Conflict: Reclaiming Healing in Education*. Oxford University Press, 2015.

INDEX

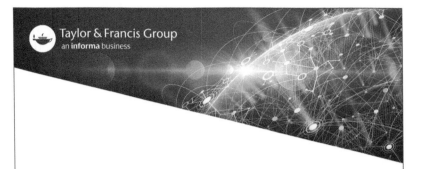

For Product Safety Concerns and Information please contact our
EU representative GPSR@taylorandfrancis.com Taylor & Francis
Verlag GmbH, Kaufingerstraße 24, 80331 München, Germany